P9-CSF-708

triple slow cooker
entertaining

triple slow cooker
entertaining

100+ Recipes & 30 Party Plans

Kathy Moore & Roxanne Wyss

Robert
ROSE

Triple Slow Cooker Entertaining
Text copyright © 2012 Electrified Cooks LLC
Photographs copyright © 2012 Robert Rose Inc.
Cover and text design copyright © 2012 Robert Rose Inc.

No part of this publication may be reproduced, stored in a retrieval system or
transmitted, in any form or by any means, without the prior written consent of the
publisher or a license from the Canadian Copyright Licensing Agency (Access
Copyright). For an Access Copyright license, visit www.accesscopyright.ca or call
toll-free: 1-800-893-5777.

For complete cataloguing information, see page 186.

Disclaimer
The recipes in this book have been carefully tested by our kitchen and our tasters. To
the best of our knowledge, they are safe and nutritious for ordinary use and users. For
those people with food or other allergies, or who have special food requirements or
health issues, please read the suggested contents of each recipe carefully and determine
whether or not they may create a problem for you. All recipes are used at the risk of the
consumer. Consumers should always consult the slow cooker manual for recommended
procedures and cooking times.

We cannot be responsible for any hazards, loss or damage that may occur as a result
of any recipe use.

For those with special needs, allergies, requirements or health problems, in the event
of any doubt, please contact your medical adviser prior to the use of any recipe.

Design and production: PageWave Graphics Inc.
Editor: Sue Sumeraj
Recipe editor: Jennifer MacKenzie
Proofreader: Sheila Wawanash
Indexer: Gillian Watts
Interior Photographs:
    Photographer: David Shaughnessy
    Food stylist: Anne Fisher
    Prop stylist: Glenda Bailey
Cover Photograph:
    Photographer: Colin Erricson
    Associate photographer: Matt Johannsson
    Food stylist: Kathryn Robertson
    Prop stylist: Charlene Erricson

Cover image: Bacon-Wrapped Chicken Bites (page 79) and Caponata Crostini (page 94)

We acknowledge the financial support of the Government of Canada through the Book
Publishing Industry Development Program (BPIDP) for our publishing activities.

Published by Robert Rose Inc.
120 Eglinton Avenue East, Suite 800, Toronto, Ontario, Canada M4P 1E2
Tel: (416) 322-6552 Fax: (416) 322-6936
www.robertrose.ca

Printed and bound in Canada

2 3 4 5 6 7 8 9 MI 20 19 18 17 16 15 14 13

Contents

Acknowledgments

The creation of this book was filled with so many supportive people, and we appreciate each one of them.

It is the love and support of our families that fuels our passion for dinner traditions and great food. We thank them for the joy they share as they taste another recipe and wash more dishes.

Roxanne's family is the light of her life. She thanks her husband, Bob Bateman, and her daughter, Grace, from the bottom of her heart. Their love, enthusiasm and constant encouragement, coupled with their appetite for taste-testing, makes her life complete.

Kathy's family, David, Laura and Amanda, are the center of her world. She cherishes their love, support, laughter and patience and wants them to know how much joy they bring her.

Thanks to publisher Bob Dees and his talented team at Robert Rose, who worked so hard to make this the best book possible. Special thanks to Sue Sumeraj, our editor; Jennifer MacKenzie, our recipe editor; Martine Quibell, publicity manager; and Marian Jarkovich, director of sales and marketing. We appreciate the wonderful creative team at PageWave Graphics, including Joseph Gisini, Kevin Cockburn and Daniella Zanchetta.

We also appreciate the creative and dedicated talent of photographer David Shaughnessy and his skilled team: Anne Fisher, Glenda Bailey and Alex Edwards. You all are awesome!

We want to thank our agents, Sally Ekus and Lisa Ekus, and the entire staff at The Lisa Ekus Group, LLC, for helping us navigate this journey and supporting us along the way.

We have been fortunate to know Bill Endres, the owner and president of Select Brands, for 30 years. We are deeply grateful to him, Eric Endres, Wes Endres and the entire Select Brands team, who are dedicated to designing, manufacturing, marketing, selling and shipping the best line of appliances.

We are also grateful to our friend Julie Bondank for her tireless work helping us test and retest these recipes.

We are blessed to have so many incredible people who support us and our work. We appreciate each one of you for your encouragement.

Most of all, we are blessed to work together as friends. Our 30-year career path has been side by side, in test kitchens and as consultants. We treasure our friendship, and that makes the journey so much more fun and rewarding.

Introduction

Let's have a party! In the past, those simple words might have invoked anxiety, but no more! Thanks to the innovative Triple Slow Cooker by Select Brands — one slow cooker with three stoneware vessels — throwing a terrific party just got much easier.

Slow cookers have been a part of our lives for a long time. We met over 30 years ago in the test kitchen of a small appliance company, where we worked daily with slow cookers. These appliances were still fairly new, and there was so much to learn. People craved slow cooker recipes, so we were kept busy developing new ones and testing product innovations. We loved working together so much, we began our consulting business, The Electrified Cooks, LLC (www.electrifiedcooks.com), and have been working together ever since.

Years later, we still love slow cooking and developing slow cooker recipes. We're delighted to share our three decades of experience, recipes and slow cooker tips with you.

We have also had the pleasure of working with Bill Endres, the owner and president of Select Brands, for over 30 years. To say he is an authority in the small appliance industry — and specifically in the slow cooker industry — is an understatement. The entire team at Select Brands works together to offer a top-quality line of slow cookers and continues to improve this appliance category.

Through the years, we have seen a slow cooker at just about every party we've attended. What buffet table is complete without a slow cooker full of meatballs, dip, chili or another tasty dish? Now, with the Triple Slow Cooker, you can offer a greater variety of delicious, hot, slow-cooked food!

We are thrilled to have the opportunity to show you how fun and easy it is to entertain using your Triple Slow Cooker. We'll share menus for all types of occasions and party themes, plus lots of recipes and tips that will make party planning a breeze.

Best of all, as the party time approaches, you'll be stress-free, knowing that the slow cooker is doing the work for you. Get ready to party!

Part 1

Entertaining with Your Triple Slow Cooker

Slow Cooker Know-How

The slow cooker is perfect for making soups, stews, sauces, dips, fondues, roasts, chilis and hot drinks, and these foods are perfect for entertaining menus! So you're sure to find all kinds of great recipes to make in your Triple Slow Cooker.

This slow cooker offers so many benefits, you will reach for it every time you entertain:

- Timing is not critical. When you're grilling steaks or burgers, or serving up a hot, freshly made pizza, you have to get the timing just right. How can you serve food hot and at the peak of perfection, even when guests are late? How can each guest at an open house enjoy top-quality food even though the party lasts for hours? The Triple Slow Cooker is the answer: it cooks three different dishes for you, then keeps each of them warm, fresh and flavorful for up to 2 hours.

- Fun for all — even you! Since a slow cooker lets you start the cooking early in the day, the kitchen can be clean and everything ready far in advance of when your guests are due to arrive. No last-minute rush. You are free to greet and enjoy your guests, and can savor the hot meal right along with everyone else.

- Compact service, yet plenty to offer. There's just one appliance to plug in, but its three 2½-quart vessels, each with separate controls, give you marvelous flexibility. You can cook your dishes on different settings, if you desire, and you can get each one going at a different time, based on how long it needs to cook, so that all of the dishes are ready simultaneously at party time.

Step-by-Step Slow Cooking

Using your Triple Slow Cooker is much like using any other slow cooker; you simply make smaller portions of each dish. If you've never used a slow cooker before, or need a refresher, here are the basic steps:

Step 1: Spray it

Spray each stoneware vessel with nonstick baking spray before filling it to make cleanup easier. This is especially important when you're cooking cheesy, sticky or sweet foods.

Step 2: Fill it

Fill one, two or all three stoneware vessels. Since they operate independently, you can fill them with different foods and set one to High and the other two to Low — or whatever combination you want. Fill each vessel about half to three-quarters full. Do not overfill.

Step 3: Cover it

Always cook with the cover on each of the stoneware vessels. Be sure the cover sits flat and is not left ajar.

Step 4: Cook it

Cook on Low or High, not on Warm. Meats and main dishes typically require 6 to 10 hours on Low, so be sure to allow plenty of time. Cook on High when you want a shorter cooking time; in general, 2 hours on Low equals about 1 hour on High.

Step 5: Forget it

Leave the slow cooker alone until it's time to check for doneness. Do not lift the lid to check on the food or to stir it — every time you lift the cover, you lose valuable heat and add to the cooking time. Certain recipes, such as dips and fondues, do need to be stirred occasionally while they're cooking, but unless a recipe specifically directs you to do so, there is no need to stir.

Step 6: Check it for doneness

Each recipe advises you on how to tell when the dish is done. Cooking time may be affected by the manufacturing tolerances, electrical voltage and other uncontrollable variables. Therefore, each recipe offers a range of cooking times. Check the dish for doneness at the minimum recommended cooking time, then continue cooking if the food is not yet done. After you've used your slow cooker a time or two, you will know if you prefer the recipes cooked to the minimum or maximum time suggested.

Getting the Best from Your Slow Cooker

Every day, but especially when entertaining, you want to serve the very best foods. The Triple Slow Cooker is a great tool for entertaining, but you are an equal part of the team. Begin with fresh, high-quality foods and cook the dishes until they are done to perfection, then serve them while they are still at the peak of quality, and you will be known for the best-tasting buffets.

Here are some more tips for getting the best results from your slow cooker.

Start early

When entertaining, it is wise to allow a little extra time instead of cutting it short. You don't want to feel flustered if the food's not done when your guests are ready to eat. If a guest is late, you can always turn the slow cooker to Warm and delay serving.

Use dried herbs and spices

Dried herbs and spices are preferred for slow cooking, as the flavor of fresh herbs seems to fade with the long cooking time. You can always punch up the flavor by adding some fresh herbs during the last few minutes of cooking.

Whole-leaf herbs or crumbled leaves will provide more intense flavor than ground herbs. Similarly, coarsely ground spices, such as pepper, are a better choice than finely ground. Keep that fine grind for a pepper shaker on the table.

For the best, most intense garlic flavor when slow cooking, we recommend dry minced (granulated) garlic. Fresh garlic and garlic powder are fine for dishes with shorter cooking times, like dips, but if you will be cooking the dish for many hours and want a definite garlic flavor, use dry minced garlic instead.

Avoid using old, stale herbs and spices. Too many people store those little bottles forever, not realizing that seasonings are perishable. Stale herbs and spices just won't add the flavor you want — and worse yet, can give an off or bitter flavor to the dish. If you've had a dried herb or spice for more than 1 year, throw it out and start over. For herbs and spices you don't use that often, buy just a small amount at a bulk or specialty store, or split the bottle or package with a friend or neighbor. If the bottle or package does not have a "use by" date printed on it, use a marker to date it yourself.

Limit the liquid

Liquids do not boil off in the slow cooker as they do on the stovetop, so most of our recipes use just a little bit of liquid. Meats can be cooked without any added liquid and certainly don't need to swim in a lot of it unless you are making a soup. You can always add liquid at the end of cooking if you wish to give the dish a thinner consistency.

If you do use too much liquid and wish to thicken the dish once it is fully cooked, there are a couple ways to do that:

- Remove the cover, turn the slow cooker to High and let the liquids boil off.
- For a soup or stew, combine 2 tbsp (30 mL) all-purpose flour or 1 tbsp (15 mL) cornstarch and 2 to 3 tbsp (30 to 45 mL) cold water to make a paste. Stir the paste into the slow cooker, cover and turn the slow cooker to High. The liquid will thicken in 15 to 30 minutes.

Taste and adjust the seasoning

You really can get the best flavor from foods that are slow-cooked, but just as with stovetop cooking, it's a good idea to taste the dish during the last few minutes of cooking and adjust the seasoning as needed. You may find that the flavor would be improved by a touch more salt or pepper, a dash of hot pepper sauce, a squeeze of lemon juice or a pinch of sugar.

Keep the food warm

Once the food is fully cooked, turn the slow cooker to Warm until you're ready to serve. To keep the food safe and at the ideal temperature, leave the lids on the stoneware vessels except when serving. A slow cooker on Warm with the lid off may drop below 140°F (60°C) into the danger zone (the temperature range — 40°F to 140°F /4°C to 60° C — in which bacteria can grow). In addition, the food will most likely dry out and become unappealing.

In general, main dishes and side dishes will stay fresh and flavorful for about 2 hours on Warm. Cheese dips, chocolate fondues and other more delicate dishes may need a bit more watching for signs of drying out or overcooking.

Keep in mind that accompanying foods on the buffet, on platters or in bowls, will also creep into the danger zone and dry out. Any perishable food left out at room temperature for 2 hours should be discarded. Never take a chance with food safety and your health. If in doubt, throw it out.

As for reheating food, the slow cooker is not recommended because the food may stay in the danger zone too long. In any case, it doesn't give good results: the food either dries out or gets mushy before it is heated through. The Triple Slow Cooker's removable stoneware vessels can go directly into the microwave oven. Cover with plastic wrap or a paper towel; do not put the lids in the microwave. Heat the food until it is steaming hot throughout, then stir or rearrange the food to be sure it is evenly hot. Return the stoneware to the slow cooker, cover and turn the slow cooker to High for 15 to 30 minutes, then turn to Warm for serving.

You can also reheat liquids, gravies or sauces in a saucepan on the stovetop: bring the liquid to a rolling boil over medium-high heat, stirring frequently so it heats evenly. To reheat food in the oven, cover it tightly and bake at 375°F (190°C) until hot (165°F/74°C) throughout. Either way, transfer the hot food to the slow cooker, cover and turn the slow cooker to High for 15 to 30 minutes, then turn to Warm for serving.

Serving a Large Crowd

We have used the Triple Slow Cooker to serve small dinner parties with just 6 to 8 guests and larger gatherings of 50 or more. For small parties, dips and appetizers can be cut in half and you can fill the slow cooker stoneware about one-third full. But what if you're serving a large crowd? Here are some suggestions on how to increase the number of servings.

For appetizers

Prepare several batches of the appetizer. When the earlier batches are done cooking, let them cool, then cover and refrigerate them. Keep the last batch warm in the slow cooker for serving right away. When you're ready to serve another batch, heat it in the microwave until steaming hot, then stir or rearrange the food to be sure it is evenly hot. Lift out and wash the stoneware vessel, fill it with the fresh food and return it to the slow cooker. Cover and turn the slow cooker to High for 15 to 30 minutes, then turn to Warm for serving.

For soups, stews or chilis

Prepare three batches — one in each stoneware vessel. For added fun and flexibility, you could make each of the batches slightly different. For example, you might prepare a mild, a medium and a hot chili. Or, if you know that some of your guests hate mushrooms and some love them, you could leave them out of one batch of stew and add them to the others. Make sure to label which is which!

Another option, if you want to use two of the stoneware vessels to serve other dishes, is to cook one large batch in a separate large slow cooker. The soup, stew and chili recipes in this book can be doubled if you're cooking them in a 6-quart slow cooker. When the dish is done, transfer it a bit at a time to the Triple Slow Cooker, keeping the remainder warm in the large slow cooker. Turn the setting on the Triple Slow Cooker to High for 30 minutes to be sure the dish stays steaming hot, then keep it set on Warm for serving.

For roasts

The Triple Slow Cooker is ideal for roasts that weigh 2 to 3 lbs (1 to 1.5 kg). If you want to cook a roast in the 3- to 5-lb (1.5 to 2.5 kg) range, use a 6-quart slow cooker instead, increasing the other ingredients in the recipe, such as vegetables, seasonings and liquids, by about half. Cook larger roasts (more than 5 lbs/2.5 kg) in the oven, using your favorite recipe.

However you cook the roast, you can use the Triple Slow Cooker to serve it. Carve the roast, fill one or more of the stoneware vessels with hot meat, cover and turn the setting to High for 30 minutes to make sure the meat is steaming hot, then set the slow cooker to Warm for serving.

If you have prepared and carved the roast ahead of time, chill the meat quickly by placing it in a shallow dish, covering it tightly and refrigerating it. Do not let it sit out at room temperature. When you're ready to serve, microwave just the amount that fits in the stoneware vessel until steaming hot. Stir or rearrange the meat, then continue microwaving until the meat reaches an internal temperature of at least 165°F (74°C). The meat should be evenly hot throughout, but be careful not to overheat, as you don't want it to dry out. Transfer the meat to the slow cooker, cover and turn the setting to High for 30 minutes, then set the slow cooker to Warm for serving.

Making Food Ahead

The lead-up to the party goes much more smoothly if you make some of the food ahead of time. Although it takes a bit of planning, the result is a more relaxed, fun event for host and guests alike. By its very nature, a slow cooker helps you avoid a last-minute rush, but there's more you can do to start getting ready even further in advance. We have sprinkled make ahead tips throughout the book, with the party menus and with the recipes, but here are some dos and don'ts to keep in mind when you're deciding what to prepare ahead.

Dos

- Wash and chop hardy vegetables, such as onions, celery and peppers, a day ahead and store them overnight in sealable plastic bags in the refrigerator.
- Measure out the seasonings, then cover them tightly or seal them in a plastic bag so they are ready to quickly sprinkle over the food the next day.
- Process bread into crumbs and store the crumbs in a sealable plastic bag.
- Shred or grate the cheese and refrigerate it in an airtight container.
- Certain dishes can be fully assembled in the stoneware vessel and refrigerated overnight. The next day, just place the stoneware in the base and turn it to the setting you want. But make sure to read the list of don'ts below for ingredients that make assembling the dish ahead a no-go.

Don'ts

- Don't peel or cut vegetables or fruits, such as potatoes, apples or avocados, that discolor quickly until just before you're ready to cook.
- Don't partially cook or brown meat, poultry or fish ahead, then finish cooking it another day. Brown it just before placing it in the slow cooker. (Ground meat can be fully cooked and refrigerated in its own separate container overnight, then stirred into the dish just before cooking.)
- Don't mix a hot cooked sauce with cooked meat or poultry, then refrigerate. Store the sauce and meat separately, so they cool quickly, then combine them in the slow cooker when you're ready to cook.
- Don't add dry rice or pasta to a slow cooker mixture in advance.
- Don't cook any dish for part of the recommended cooking time, interrupt it and finish cooking the next day.

Ready, Set, Party!

Entertaining at home offers many benefits. You control the flavor and freshness of the food, and can accommodate your guests' dietary restrictions. You don't have to deal with crowds of people — outside of the ones you've invited, of course. You create the ambience, setting the tone for the mood of the party, whether you're planning on hosting a quiet gathering or a rowdy bash. As the host, you are in charge. But don't let that intimidate you — we'll walk you through everything you need to know to plan and execute your menu and create a fun and memorable celebration.

Planning Your Party

The first step is to make a plan, deciding what type of party to throw, when to hold it (both the date and the time of day) and how many people to invite. These choices will help you determine what type of food you're going to serve and how much of it you're going to need.

What is the reason for the party?

Is the party for your child's birthday, with all of the guests under the age of 10? Is it a gathering of your extended family to celebrate a holiday? Is it an afternoon bridal shower for women only? Or is it for a group of sports fans to watch the big game and cheer your team on to victory? There are lots of great reasons to throw a party, and the reason will suggest the theme, menu, decorations, number of guests and activities.

On pages 22–51, we give you party plans for 30 different themes, including the menu, tips to make the event easy and decorating suggestions. Remember, you can mix and match the food suggestions to accommodate your specific party and personal preferences.

When is the party?

For some events, such as a New Year's Eve or graduation party, you will want to issue the invitations a month or more in advance. For a family reunion where travel plans are required, some families set the date a year in advance. When gathering to watch your team in the basketball finals, you might plan just a few days or a week in advance — and the date will be set for you.

What time of day is the party?

Do you want to host a brunch? An afternoon party? A dinner party? An after-dinner soirée? The time of day often dictates whether you'll be serving a full meal, heavy appetizers or fun snacks. It will also help narrow down your menu options: you're bound to make different choices for a brunch than for a cocktail party!

You'll definitely want to set a start time for your event, but you might consider adding an end time as well. This gives your guests an idea of your expectations and encourages them not to overstay their welcome. For a children's party, it also lets their parents know when to pick the kids up. Of course, when the time comes, if everybody — including you — is having too much fun to call it quits, you can always just ignore the end time and invite everyone to stay longer.

How many people will you invite?

"The more the merrier" is a common mindset, but be realistic about your limits when compiling your guest list. How many people will your home accommodate? For a sit-down dinner party, the number might be determined by how many people will fit around the table. For a casual cocktail party, where people will be milling about, you have much more flexibility. For a kids' party, consider not only how many kids your party area will hold, but also how many you are willing to be responsible for at one time.

Planning Your Menu

Look back at your party plan: the theme, time of day and number of guests will all affect your menu choices. You'll also want to consider the ages and preferences of your guests. Children tend to like foods that are familiar, and most kids don't care for spicy foods. Adults may be more adventurous, although there always seems to be one conservative diner at every party. Some guests may have dietary restrictions or food allergies that must be taken into account; others may have ethical or religious preferences that should be honored.

The easiest way to accommodate a wide range of preferences and tastes is to offer a variety of foods. Variety is not just the spice of life, it is the template for a great menu. Offer some spicy and some milder dishes. Balance cold salads with hot entrées. Offer a rich appetizer and a light dessert. All of the dishes on your menu should support the theme, but avoid duplicating the same ingredients in each dish.

Keep in mind that you don't need to make everything on the menu yourself. Balance your time by purchasing a salad, a cheese platter, a veggie tray, a fruit salad and/or a bakery dessert. And if others offer to help, let them!

Prepping for the Party

Do as much of the preparation as you can in advance so that you're not rushing frantically around trying to get everything done on the day of the party. There's nothing worse than realizing at the very last minute that you've forgotten a crucial detail. The more you're able to get done early, the less chance you'll be in a panic right as the party's about to start.

- A week or so in advance, make a list of everything you'll need to purchase to complete every dish on your menu. In addition to the ingredients that go into the dish, plan the garnishes. What will make the dish look stunning? A sprig or sprinkling of fresh herbs, citrus slices, a dollop of sour cream or a spoonful of colorful jam may be what a dish needs to go from ho-hum to wow!
- Shop for pantry items and staples several days in advance. Purchase perishable items the day before.
- Double-check your supply of beverages the day before. Do you have enough coffee, tea, sugar, creamer, lemon? Is the soda or beer chilled? Is the wine at the proper temperature? Do you have plenty of ice?
- Remember, to round out your menu, you will be serving some foods that are not cooked in the slow cooker, and many of these can be prepared the day before. Salads can be assembled and dressings mixed, ready to toss together just before the party. Cake or brownies can be baked. Chilled dips or sauces can be made.

- Plan and set the buffet table a day or two in advance. Iron the tablecloth, set out the napkins, serving dishes, glasses and utensils, and fill the salt and pepper shakers.

Setting Up the Buffet

First, decide where the slow cooker will sit. It should be the star of the buffet, so give it center stage on the table if you can. But remember that it needs to plug into an electrical outlet, so that practical consideration may dictate its placement. If you choose to use an extension cord, do so very cautiously. The marked electrical rating of the extension cord should be at least as great as the rating of the slow cooker. Make sure the cord is not a trip hazard and is not draped over the tabletop, where it can be pulled on by children.

The arrangement of everything else on the table is determined by traffic flow. The plates come first, followed by appetizers and other first-course foods, then salads and other cold dishes. Next come the hot foods — or more specifically, the slow cooker filled with three hot dishes — followed by accompaniments, condiments and sauces. The flatware and napkins are placed after the food so diners don't have to juggle them as they fill their plates. Desserts and beverages are often last; for convenience, you might place them at a separate table or even in another room.

Remember, we eat with our eyes first. Plan the tablecloth, centerpiece, candles and decorations as integral parts of the buffet, not afterthoughts. Create different heights on the table with cake tiers, footed bowls or plates, or platters placed on inverted bowls or glasses. And make good use of color — not just in the food, but in the linens and plates and even for the tiers. (Tip: fill a clear glass bowl with multicolored candy, place a platter on top and voila — you have just made a colorful tier.)

Party Plans

New Year's Eve

Celebrate in style at home. Invite lots of friends, enjoy savory dips and appetizers and toast the arrival of the new year.

Cheesy Black-Eyed Pea Dip (page 58)
Tortilla chips or corn chips
Gruyère and Wild Rice Dip (page 63)
Toasted baguette slices and crackers
Artichoke and Goat Cheese Crostini (page 93)
Vegetable crudités
Wine, cocktails and nonalcoholic cocktails
Champagne and sparkling grape juice
Coffee

Countdown to the Party

- **2 to 3 hours ahead:** Start the Cheesy Black-Eyed Pea Dip.
- **1 to 2 hours ahead:** Toast the baguette slices.
- **1½ hours ahead:** Start the Artichoke and Goat Cheese Crostini.
- **1 hour ahead:** Start the Gruyère and Wild Rice Dip.

Make Ahead Suggestions

- Assemble the Cheesy Black-Eyed Pea Dip the day before (see page 58 for full details).
- Assemble the Gruyère and Wild Rice Dip early in the day. Cover and refrigerate until cooking time.
- For the crostini, assemble the artichoke mixture through step 3 early in the day. Cover and refrigerate until cooking time.

Completing the Menu

- Place plenty of chips, toasted baguette slices and crackers in baskets near the slow cooker.
- Arrange vegetable crudités on a platter. Those counting calories will thank you for the lower-fat alternative.

- Stock plenty of beverages — both alcohol and nonalcoholic — and keep an extra bag of ice in the freezer.
- Add a bowl of mints in anticipation of the midnight kiss!

Decorations and Activities

- Blue and silver is a pretty color scheme for this event. Silver wrapping paper makes a festive runner — just unroll it down the center of the table and tape the ends underneath. Make a centerpiece by stacking blue and silver Christmas ornaments in your prettiest glass bowl.
- Set clocks at various heights around the food on the buffet table. Choose clocks of different sizes and looks. Be sure they are all set to the same time — or set each one to a different time zone.
- Light lots of candles and dim the lights.
- Roll up silverware in a napkin, then tie each end with metallic ribbons so the roll looks like a firecracker.
- Challenge your guests to write down fun, crazy, realistic or novel resolutions to share throughout the evening.

Chinese New Year

Serve up both great food and good luck to celebrate this holiday in traditional Chinese style. Include lots of red — a symbol of good luck — in your decorations.

Crab Rangoon Dip (page 64)

Crisp fried wonton wrappers

Asian Chicken Wings (page 78)

Asian-Style Ribs (page 81)

Fortune cookies

Hot green tea, jasmine tea or oolong tea

Countdown to the Party

- **8 to 10 hours ahead:** Start the Asian-Style Ribs if you're cooking them on Low (if cooking on High, start $4\frac{1}{2}$ to $5\frac{1}{2}$ hours ahead).

- **4 to 5 hours ahead:** Start the Asian Chicken Wings if you're cooking them on Low (if cooking on High, start 2 to $2\frac{1}{2}$ hours ahead). Remember to broil them until crisp just before the party begins.

- **1 hour ahead:** Broil the ribs, place them in one stoneware, cover and turn to Warm. Wash out the other stoneware used to cook the ribs, then start the Crab Rangoon Dip.

Make Ahead Suggestions

- Assemble the dip the day before (see page 64 for full details).

- Deep-fry the wonton wrappers the day before (see page 64 for full details).

- Prepare the wings for cooking the night before (see page 78 for full details).

Completing the Menu

- Plan on a large basket or bowl of the fried wontons to serve with the Crab Rangoon Dip, as everyone will love them. For a very large gathering, call a local Chinese restaurant and order a large amount of crisp wonton strips.

- Order a supply of fortune cookies from a local Chinese restaurant.

- Brew the tea, then keep the pot warm by placing it on an electric warming tray.

Decorations and Activities

- Cover the table with a black tablecloth, then scatter it with gold confetti. Arrange a bowl of oranges or tangerines — which symbolize luck and wealth — as a centerpiece.

- Light red and gold candles.

- Place red and black balloons, tied with gold ribbon, in large clusters around the room, or let them float loose on the ceiling. If you live in a house, tie several balloons outside to set the stage.

- String flower garlands over the mantel and doorways.

- Scatter Chinese takeout boxes around the room. Fill them to overflowing with wonton strips, fortune cookies or favors.

- Cut out drawings of the animal symbol that represents the year ahead on the Chinese calendar. Tape them to your windows or scatter them on the buffet table.

- Write out lots of fortunes, personalized for your guests, their interests and your locale, and have everyone guess who they might be intended for.

Super Bowl Party

When you gather your friends to watch the big game, you want the food to score big, yet be so easy that you don't miss a minute of the action.

Fiery Hot Wings (page 75)

Tangy Meatballs (page 91)

Champion Chili (page 106)

Sour cream, shredded cheese, chopped onions, sliced jalapeño peppers

Popcorn, tortilla chips with salsa

Brownies

Beer and soft drinks

Countdown to the Party

- **6 to 8 hours ahead:** Start the Champion Chili if you're cooking it on Low (if cooking on High, start 3 to 4 hours ahead). Allow time to brown the beef first if you haven't done this ahead.

- **4 to 5 hours ahead:** Start the Fiery Hot Wings if you're cooking them on Low (if cooking on High, start 2 to $2\frac{1}{2}$ hours ahead). Remember to broil them until crisp just before the party begins.

- **3 to 4 hours ahead:** Start the Tangy Meatballs if you're cooking them on Low (if cooking on High, start $1\frac{1}{2}$ to 2 hours ahead). Allow time for forming and baking them first if you haven't done this ahead.

Make Ahead Suggestions

- Prepare the wings for cooking the night before (see page 75 for full details).

- Form and bake the meatballs the day before (see page 91 for full details).

- Assemble the chili the day before (see page 106 for full details).

Completing the Menu

- Set out bowls of sour cream, cheese, onions and jalapeños on the buffet table and encourage guests to top their chili just the way they like it.

- Everyone likes to munch and snack while watching a game, so set bowls of popcorn, tortilla chips and salsa conveniently around the room.

- Pick up some brownies at a local bakery so the party ends on a sweet note no matter who wins the game.

- Keep plenty of beer and soft drinks on ice.

- For added fun, serve beers, specialty cheeses or famous foods associated with the towns the competing teams are from.

Decorations

- Cover the table in green and place tape strips evenly down the table to mark out "yard lines." Pick up napkins in each team color and alternate them on the table.

- Set out pompoms and foam footballs. Start the party at the door by tying a pompom on the handle or hoisting a football flag nearby.

- Rearrange the TV room as needed so everyone has a clear view of the television. Set up the buffet in the kitchen or on a table nearby.

Valentine's Day

Plan an elegant dinner party for a few close friends. It's the perfect time to set the table with your best dishes and light the candles.

Hearts of Palm Dip (page 62)

Crackers or toasted baguette slices

Beef Burgundy (page 120)

Hot cooked noodles

Winter Salad (page 161)

Elegant Chocolate Fondue (page 164)

Strawberries, pineapple cubes, banana slices, dried apricot halves, pirouette cookies, cubes of pound cake or angel cake

Red wine, Champagne, sparkling water

Countdown to the Party

- **7 to 9 hours ahead:** Start the Beef Burgundy if you're cooking it on Low (if cooking on High, start $3\frac{1}{2}$ to $4\frac{1}{2}$ hours ahead).

- **1 hour ahead:** Start the Hearts of Palm Dip.

- **$1\frac{1}{2}$ hours before you want dessert:** Start the Elegant Chocolate Fondue.

Make Ahead Suggestions

- Assemble the dip the night before (see page 62 for full details).

- For the Beef Burgundy, cut the beef into cubes, chop the onion and slice the carrot the day before. Store the beef and vegetables in separate containers in the refrigerator.

- For the salad, wash the greens, cook and crumble the bacon, toast the walnuts and prepare the dressing the day before. Cover and refrigerate each separately overnight. Bring the dressing to room temperature and whisk well before use. Do not toss the salad until just before serving.

Completing the Menu

- For the dip, select "gourmet" crackers at a specialty or gourmet shop, or purchase the freshest baguette you can find.

- Cook the noodles at the last minute — about 10 minutes before you wish to sit down for dinner — and just until al dente.

- For fondue dippers, set out a variety of fresh fruit, as well as crisp cookies and cubes of pound cake or angel food cake.

- A Pinot Noir, Shiraz, Bordeaux or Burgundy would complement the rich flavors of the Beef Burgundy. Add chilled Champagne for a fun toast. To add to the French feel, offer both "still" and "fizzy" water.

Decorations

- Your best black or white tablecloth will provide the perfect backdrop for red roses, scattered rose petals and candelabras.

- Write out the menu in French and place a white menu card at each place setting.

- Use lighting to evoke Paris — the City of Lights. If you live in a house, light the path to your door with luminaries or outdoor lights. Place a small replica of the Eiffel Tower, covered in twinkling Christmas tree lights, near the front door.

- Scatter pictures of Paris around the room, and greet your guests with *"Bonjour."*

Mardi Gras

Celebrate Mardi Gras in true New Orleans style. Gather your friends and laissez les bons temps rouler.

Cajun Smoked Sausage Po' Boys (page 127)

Red Beans and Rice (page 152)

Bananas Foster (page 172)

Ice cream

King cake

Hurricanes, punch

Countdown to the Party

- **5 to 7 hours ahead:** Start the Red Beans and Rice if you're cooking it on Low (if cooking on High, start 2 to 3 hours ahead).

- **4 to 6 hours ahead:** Start the Cajun Smoked Sausage Po' Boy mixture if you're cooking it on Low (if cooking on High, start 2 to 3 hours ahead).

- **30 to 60 minutes before you want dessert:** Start the Bananas Foster as your guests arrive, or even as you begin to eat dinner, so it is ready for dessert.

Make Ahead Suggestions

- Assemble the po' boy mixture the night before (see page 127 for full details).

- For the Red Beans and Rice, chop the sausage, celery and onions the night before. Store the sausage and vegetables in separate containers in the refrigerate.

Completing the Menu

- Scoops of vanilla ice cream make the perfect backdrop for the bananas Foster. To make serving ice cream to a crowd easier, line a baking sheet with parchment paper. Place scoops of ice cream on the tray and set the tray in the freezer so the scoops can refreeze.

- King cake is a tradition for Mardi Gras. A prize, such as a small baby (to represent Baby Jesus), a coin or a pecan, is often hidden in the sweet, yeast-leavened cake. Whoever finds the prize in their piece is named king or queen of the party and must supply the cake at the next year's celebration. Ask your local bakery if they sell king cake or can make one for you. Caution partygoers to keep an eye out for the prize, so no one accidentally chokes on it.

- Hurricanes are a popular rum-based fruit drink served in New Orleans. Make a pitcher, following your favorite recipe or using a mix, and serve in icy tall glasses. For a nonalcoholic option, make a punch from pineapple juice and passion fruit juice; serve over ice.

Decorations

- The colors of Mardi Gras are traditionally purple, gold and green, so use those colors in the tablecloth, dishes, candles and flowers. Complete the buffet table with decorative masks.

- Tie balloons to the front door and greet each guest with inexpensive beads.

- For added fun, encourage guests to come in costume.

- Play jazz or music of the Louisiana bayous.

Oscar Viewing

Host an award-winning party with your own red carpet event. Encourage your guests to wear their finest so they are ready for the paparazzi.

Scrumptious Sweet and Spicy Nuts (page 96)

Classic Cheese Fondue (page 70)

Crusty French bread cubes, vegetable crudités, roasted new potatoes

Amaretto Cream Fondue (page 169)

Cubes of pound cake or angel food cake, strawberries, long-stemmed maraschino cherries or fresh sweet cherries, shortbread cookies

Champagne or sparkling juice

Coffee

Countdown to the Party

- **2 to 2½ hours ahead:** Start the Scrumptious Sweet and Spicy Nuts.

- **30 minutes ahead:** Start the Classic Cheese Fondue.

- **30 to 60 minutes before you want dessert:** Start the Amaretto Cream Fondue.

Make Ahead Suggestions

- Cut the vegetables for dipping in the cheese fondue the day before.

- If serving cake cubes with the dessert fondue, bake the cake the day before so it will be cool and ready to cut into cubes. Of course, you can always pick one up at a local bakery.

Completing the Menu

- Surround the fondues with a wide array of dippers.

- Pour Champagne or sparkling juice to toast the winners.

Decorations

- Rearrange the TV room as needed so everyone has a clear view of the television. Set up the buffet in the kitchen or on a table nearby.

- Unroll inexpensive red fabric on the path leading to your front door, and have award-winning theme songs playing as your guests arrive. Greet guests with the snap of a camera — and be sure to turn on the flash. Print out the pictures by evening's end so each guest leaves with his or her photo.

Final Four

The action on the court is fast-paced and competitive, and no one will want to miss a minute. With this menu, guests can serve themselves, then settle in to watch the game.

Bacon Cheeseburger Dip (page 68)
Tortilla chips or corn chips, vegetable crudités
Beer-Braised Cocktail Sausages (page 83)
Buffalo Sloppy Joe Sliders (page 85)
Cupcakes
Microbrews, iced tea, soft drinks

Countdown to the Party

- **5 to 7 hours ahead:** Start the Buffalo Sloppy Joe mixture if you're cooking it on Low (if cooking on High, start $2\frac{1}{2}$ to $3\frac{1}{2}$ hours ahead). Allow time to brown the beef first if you haven't done this ahead.

- **2 to 4 hours ahead:** Start the Beer-Braised Cocktail Sausages if you're cooking them on Low (if cooking on High, start 1 to 2 hours ahead).

- **$2\frac{1}{2}$ hours ahead:** Start the Bacon Cheeseburger Dip. Allow time to brown the beef first if you haven't done this ahead.

Make Ahead Suggestions

- Cook the bacon for the dip the day before. Let it cool, then crumble and refrigerate it in an airtight container.

- Brown the ground beef for the sliders and the dip the day before. Refrigerate it in an airtight container.

Completing the Menu

- Offer a tray of fresh vegetable crudités, ready for dipping, along with bowls of chips.

- Frost the cupcakes in team colors.

- Serve foods, beverages or microbrews associated with the towns the competing teams are from.

Decorations

- Show your support for your favorite team by using their colors — or give equal time to each team.

- Stick silhouettes of basketball players on the windows. Hang a foam basketball hoop on a doorway and pass out foam basketballs. Paint a scoreboard on poster board to hang above the buffet table. If you can tolerate the noise, give each guest a referee whistle.

Soup and Salad Buffet

Whatever the occasion — a sorority meeting, a neighborhood get-together or a gathering of girlfriends — with this easy menu, you'll have time to enjoy the food and the laughter.

Strawberry Spinach Salad (page 160)

Winter Salad (page 161)

French Onion Soup (page 98)

Roasted Tomato Basil Soup (page 99)

Crusty rolls with butter

Peach Crumble (page 175)

Coffee, iced tea, lemonade

Countdown to the Party

- **$6^1/_2$ to $8^1/_2$ hours ahead:** Start the French Onion Soup if you haven't made it ahead.

- **$5^1/_2$ to $7^1/_2$ hours ahead:** Start the Roasted Tomato Basil Soup if you haven't made it ahead.

- **4 to 6 hours ahead:** Start the Peach Crumble if you're cooking it on Low (if cooking on High, start 2 to 3 hours ahead).

- **1 to 2 hours ahead:** Purée the Roasted Tomato Basil Soup and return it to the slow cooker.

- **30 minutes ahead:** Add the remaining ingredients to the French Onion Soup.

Make Ahead Suggestions

- For the salads, wash the greens and prepare each of the salad dressings the day before. Slice the red onion, toast the almond and hard-cook the eggs for the Strawberry Spinach salad. Cook and crumble the bacon and toast the walnuts for the Winter salad. Cover and refrigerate each separately overnight. Bring the Winter Salad dressing to room temperature and whisk well before use. Do not toss the salads until just before serving.

- Prepare both soups through step 2 the day before and refrigerate overnight. About an hour before the party starts, working with one soup at a time, microwave soup on High for 10 to 12 minutes or until steaming hot. Set the stoneware in the slow cooker and cook on High for 30 minutes, then proceed with step 3 of each recipe.

- Toast the pecans so they are ready to use in the Peach Crumble.

Completing the Menu

- Pick up fresh, crusty rolls and be sure to make plenty of coffee, iced tea and lemonade.

Decorations

- Capture the joy of friendship in your decorations, using fun, bright colors and a simple, inviting look.

- Use your china and tea service — your girlfriends are worth it. Mix and match sets until you have enough to serve everyone.

- Add daisies or garden flowers in small vases.

Come for Coffee

Invite your neighbors over to welcome newcomers to the neighborhood. Or invite some friends over to hang out for the afternoon. The Triple Slow Cooker allows you to offer three different types of coffee, and refills will always be hot!

Gingerbread Latte (page 184)

Caramel Latte (page 183)

Vanilla Latte (page 182)

Regular coffee, decaffeinated coffee, tea

Cookies, muffins or scones

Countdown to the Party

- **$2\frac{1}{4}$ to $3\frac{1}{4}$ hours ahead:** To have plenty of coffee for the three different lattes, brew a full pot of coffee in a 12-cup coffeemaker.

- **2 to 3 hours ahead:** Start the Gingerbread Latte.

- **2 hours ahead:** Start the Caramel Latte.

- **$1\frac{1}{2}$ hours ahead:** Start the Vanilla Latte.

Completing the Menu

- Just before the party, make another pot of coffee for those who want it black. It's also a good idea to offer decaffeinated coffee — make sure to label it so everyone knows which one it is. For those who don't care for coffee, consider offering a selection of hot teas and perhaps a cold beverage, such as lemonade or ice water with lemon twists.

- Make your favorite cookies, muffins or scones (or any other sweet treat), or pick up some at the bakery, to offer with the coffee. If you choose scones, set out little pots of jam nearby.

- For fun, dip spoons in melted chocolate to make tasty stirrers. Place chocolate chips or white or chocolate candy coating wafers in a small, deep microwave-safe glass bowl. Microwave on High in 30-second intervals, stirring after each, until melted. Dip the spoons (either metal or plastic) into the chocolate, covering the bowl of the spoon evenly, and tap gently to allow excess to drip off. Place spoons on a tray lined with waxed paper to set (or insert the handles into a block of Styrofoam.)

- Set out milk, cream, sugar cubes and flavored syrups.

Decorations

- Let your coffee mugs or cups guide the other decorations. Cover the table in a festive cloth and choose fresh flowers in colors that complement the colors in the mugs.

- Do you have mismatched vintage coffee cups? This is the perfect opportunity to use them!

- For a casual gathering and an instant conversation starter, ask each guest to bring a favorite coffee cup or mug — and to be prepared to explain why it is a favorite.

Teen Time

Your house will become the favorite spot for your teen's friends to gather when you serve meals like this one. It's easy on you — and easy for them to serve themselves.

Queso Dip (page 56)

Tortilla chips

Beef and Salsa Taco Filling (page 124)

Warm taco shells or flour tortillas

Shredded lettuce, chopped tomatoes, shredded cheese, guacamole, salsa and sour cream

Apple Crisp (page 174)

Ice cream

Soft drinks, ice water

Countdown to the Party

- **4 to 6 hours ahead:** Start the Beef and Salsa Taco Filling if you're cooking it on Low (if cooking on High, start 2 to 3 hours ahead).

- **4 to 5 hours ahead:** Start the Apple Crisp if you're cooking it on Low (if cooking on High, start 2 to $2\frac{1}{2}$ hours ahead). Allow about 20 minutes to peel and slice the apples first.

- **2 to 3 hours ahead:** Start the Queso Dip.

Make Ahead Suggestions

- Assemble the dip the day before (see page 56 for full details).

- Assemble the taco filling the day before (see page 124 for full details).

Completing the Menu

- Set out a big bowl of tortilla chips for dipping, and don't forget a plate of taco shells.

- With a casual, Mexican-inspired dinner like this one, the toppings add to the fun and round out the meal. Set out bowls of shredded lettuce, chopped tomatoes, shredded cheese, guacamole, salsa and sour cream. If desired, add sliced jalapeño peppers, sliced olives, chopped onions or other favorite toppings.

- Apple crisp is perfect with a scoop of ice cream, so be sure to stock the freezer.

- Have plenty of ice-cold soft drinks on hand.

Decorations and Activities

- Cover the table with yards of denim. It is easy to wash afterwards, yet provides a beautiful backdrop for the luscious food and colorful bowls of condiments.

- Fill a piñata with candy, then set it at the back of the buffet table. Don't tell anyone it is filled with candy — just let the teens break it open and send handfuls of candy home with them.

Adult Birthday Party

Celebrate a friend or family member with a fun birthday party. This easy menu will handle a crowd.

Chicken Enchilada Dip (page 65)

Tortilla chips

Slow-Smoked Beef Brisket (page 118)

Crusty rolls or toasted buns, barbecue sauce

Coleslaw

Coconut White Chocolate Fondue (page 166)

Cubes of angel food cake or pound cake, strawberries, banana slices, pineapple cubes, graham crackers

Soft drinks, iced tea, beer

Countdown to the Party

- **5 to 6 hours ahead:** Start the Slow-Smoked Beef Brisket if you haven't roasted it ahead.
- **2 to 3 hours ahead:** Start the Chicken Enchilada Dip and the Coconut White Chocolate Fondue.

Make Ahead Suggestions

- Assemble the dip the day before (see page 65 for full details).
- Roast the brisket the day before (see page 118 for full details).
- If serving cake cubes with the fondue, bake the cake the day before so it will be cool and ready to cut into cubes. Of course, you can always pick one up at a local bakery.

Completing the Menu

- Set out a big bowl of tortilla chips for dipping, along with a tray of crusty rolls or toasted buns and a bowl of barbecue sauce for the brisket.
- Follow the lead of many Kansas City restaurants and serve coleslaw with your brisket. Use your favorite recipe or toss together packaged shredded cabbage and bottled dressing.
- Arrange a lavish array of dippers on a large tray for the dessert fondue.
- Buy an extra bag or two of ice so you will have plenty to keep the beverages cold.
- Create a specialty drink and name it for the birthday honoree. Keep it simple — for example, combine a bottled juice blend with lemon-lime soda or ginger ale — but use a special glass filled with crushed ice and garnish the drink with a skewer of berries so it looks fantastic.

Decorations

- Create a photo timeline of the honoree, capturing special ages and events. Add lots of balloons and streamers.
- If you have time to go all out, model your decorations after what was in vogue in the year the honoree was born. Or set up vignettes of stages in the honoree's life: a favorite childhood game, music from his or her teen years, travel memorabilia and so on.

Kid's Birthday Party

Create a fun event by building around a theme your child loves, but make things easy on yourself by sticking to a simple menu and decorations. Another plus for this menu: adults will also enjoy the food. You might want to double the fondue so there is plenty for all of the guests.

Sloppy Joe Sliders (page 84)

Family Favorite Macaroni and Cheese (page 147)

Carrot sticks with ranch dressing

Simply Scrumptious Chocolate Fondue (page 165)

Graham crackers, large marshmallows, strawberries, banana slices, cubes of pound cake or angel food cake

Chilled juice boxes, milk and flavored milk, soft drinks

Countdown to the Party

- **5 to 7 hours ahead:** Start the Sloppy Joe mixture if you're cooking it on Low (if cooking on High, start $2\frac{1}{2}$ to $3\frac{1}{2}$ hours ahead). Allow time to brown the beef first if you haven't done this ahead.

- **2 hours ahead:** Start the Family Favorite Macaroni and Cheese.

- **1 hour ahead:** Start the Simply Scrumptious Chocolate Fondue.

Make Ahead Suggestions

- Brown the ground beef and combine the sauce mixture for the sliders the day before (see page 84 for full details).

- If serving cake cubes with the fondue, bake the cake the day before so it will be cool and ready to cut into cubes. Of course, you can always pick one up at a local bakery.

Completing the Menu

- Sliders are often served as a trendy appetizer, but they are the perfect size for children, and many bakeries are now offering these smaller buns. If you don't see them, ask the bakery manager to order them or bake them for you. Of course, if they're not available, you can serve the sloppy joe mixture on regular buns.

- Kids don't mind eating carrots when they're served in stick form, with ranch dressing to dip them into.

- Surround the fondue with kid-friendly dippers. Since every child likes to blow out the candles, place them in a pound cake or angel food cake, let the birthday boy or girl blow the candles out, then quickly cut the cake into cubes.

- Individual juice boxes or single-serve cartons of milk can be iced in a large tub so they are easy to serve, fun to drink and will keep spills to a minimum.

Decorations and Activities

- Party stores offer a variety of goods based on themes that are popular with children. To keep expenses down, pick just one or two items from the themed merchandise and purchase other necessary items in complementary colors.

- Change up a traditional game to reflect the theme: instead of a guessing game, play baseball trivia; instead of charades, play Guess the Action Figure.

- Choose a craft that can double as the party favors. For example, the kids can decorate tiaras or color superhero masks.

Overnight Guests

Hosting overnight guests is such fun. If you're planning a day filled with activities, you'll want to serve a good breakfast to start the day off right. This menu makes it easy to serve everyone a hot breakfast while keeping the morning relaxed.

Overnight Fruited Oatmeal (page 140)

Old-Fashioned Warm Fruit Compote (page 159)

Biscuits and Gravy (page 138)

Orange juice, coffee

Countdown to the Party

- **The night before:** Start the Overnight Fruited Oatmeal and the Old-Fashioned Warm Fruit Compote just before you retire. The first one up should turn them to Warm.

- **In the morning:** Make the Biscuits and Gravy, then keep the gravy warm for all to enjoy — even those who sleep late. (To reheat a biscuit for a late riser, wrap it in paper towels and microwave on High for 30 seconds or until warm.)

Completing the Menu

- Just add fresh orange juice and a pot of hot coffee and you are ready.

- For a brunch a little later in the day, serve Sausage Hash Brown Casserole (page 137) instead of one of the other dishes, or serve one of the lattes (pages 182–184).

Decorations

- Set out an array of city guides, local maps and the local newspaper so your guests can become familiar with the locale. Otherwise, there is no need for decorations, although bright colors and fresh flowers will set the pace for a happy day ahead.

- If hosting your guests for a holiday or religious celebration, incorporate colors and decorations that are traditional for the event.

Italian Dinner

Italian foods are so universally popular, you can serve this menu year-round and for any event.

Artichoke and Spinach Dip (page 61)
Hot garlic bread or bread sticks
Italian Meatballs (page 86) with Marinara Sauce (page 111)
Pasta
Italian Salad (page 162)
Cannoli, tiramisu, gelato or spumoni
Chianti, espresso

Countdown to the Party

- **8 to 11 hours ahead:** Start the Marinara Sauce if you're cooking it on Low (if cooking on High, start $3\frac{1}{2}$ to 5 hours ahead).

- **3 to 4 hours ahead:** Start the Italian Meatballs if you're cooking them on Low (if cooking on High, start 1 to $1\frac{1}{2}$ hours ahead). Allow time for forming and browning them first if you haven't done this ahead.

- **1 to 2 hours ahead:** Start the Artichoke and Spinach Dip.

Make Ahead Suggestions

- Assemble the dip and the marinara sauce the day before (see pages 61 and 111 for full details).

- Form and brown the meatballs the day before (see page 86 for full details).

- For the salad, wash the greens, slice the onions, grate the Parmesan and prepare the dressing the day before. Cover and refrigerate each separately overnight. Bring the dressing to room temperature and whisk well before use. Do not toss the salad until just before serving.

Completing the Menu

- Set out a basket of hot garlic bread or bread sticks for dipping.

- For the pasta, we suggest a sturdy tubular pasta, such as rigatoni or ziti, or a fun shape, such as farfalle (bow ties). Long pasta, such as spaghetti, would be great with the meatballs and sauce, but must be very freshly cooked when served so it doesn't stick together; rigatoni and ziti are more forgiving. Slightly undercook the pasta, then keep it in a colander, ready to dip into boiling water to reheat and moisten it as you serve.

- For a traditional Italian dessert, pick up cannoli or tiramisu from a nearby restaurant, or gelato or spumoni from the grocery store.

- Serve Chianti or another Italian wine with the meal, and espresso with dessert.

Decorations

- Embrace the cliché and use a red-and-white-checked tablecloth to cover the buffet table and wine bottles to hold your candles. Alternatively, decorate the table in red, white and green — the colors of the Italian flag.

- Hang an Italian flag and put up iconic Italian travel posters or photographs.

- If the night is warm, gather outside by candlelight and pretend you're in Tuscany.

- Be sure to play appropriate background music.

Cinco de Mayo

Transform a spring evening into a Mexican fiesta with easy but fantastic food.

Tex-Mex Spinach Dip (page 59)

Tortilla chips

Chipotle Beef with Fresh Tomato Salsa (page 116)

Chicken con Queso (page 133)

Warm tortillas

Pico de gallo, guacamole, sour cream, shredded cheese, diced tomatoes, chopped onions or green onions, sliced jalapeño peppers, sliced black olives

Margaritas, beer, limeade

Countdown to the Party

- **9 to 11 hours ahead:** Start the Chipotle Beef if you're cooking it on Low (if cooking on High, start $4\frac{1}{2}$ to $5\frac{1}{2}$ hours ahead).
- **$5\frac{1}{2}$ to $6\frac{1}{2}$ hours ahead:** Start the Chicken con Queso if you're cooking it on Low (if cooking on High, start 3 to $3\frac{1}{2}$ hours ahead).
- **1 hour ahead:** Start the Tex-Mex Spinach Dip.

Make Ahead Suggestions

- Assemble the dip the day before (see page 59 for full details).
- For the Chipotle Beef, prepare the Tomato Salsa the day before.

Completing the Menu

- Set out a big bowl of tortilla chips for dipping.
- Warm tortillas by wrapping them in foil and heating them in a 300°F (150°C) oven for 10 to 15 minutes or until warm. For easy serving, roll up each tortilla and wrap individually in foil. Arrange the foil-wrapped tortillas in a basket and cover with a colorful napkin.

- Arrange bowls of the condiments for the Chicken con Queso near the basket of tortillas.
- Make pitchers of margaritas and put beer on ice. Set out pitchers of frosty limeade and ice water for those who prefer not to consume alcohol. Make sure to label which pitchers contain margaritas and which contain limeade.

Decorations

- Cinco de Mayo calls for hot, bright colors. Cover the table in red and set an inexpensive sombrero or piñata in the center.
- For added fun, if you can handle the noise, add a set or two of maracas to the table.

Derby Day

Invite your friends over to enjoy Southern cuisine and watch the Kentucky Derby, held on the first Saturday in May. Encourage everyone to wear "Derby attire," including those gorgeous hats.

Strawberry Spinach Salad (page 160)

Hot Browns (page 134)

Parmesan Herb Potato Casserole (page 144)

Roasted asparagus

Mint chip ice cream

Hot Fudge Sauce (page 171)

Lemonade, sweet iced tea, mint juleps

Countdown to the Party

- **$3\frac{1}{4}$ to $4\frac{1}{4}$ hours ahead:** Start the Parmesan Herb Potato Casserole.

- **$3\frac{1}{2}$ to 4 hours ahead:** Start roasting the turkey breast for the Hot Browns if you haven't roasted it ahead.

- **30 to 60 minutes ahead:** Start the Hot Fudge Sauce and start cooking the roasted turkey in the Mornay Sauce.

Make Ahead Suggestions

- For the salad, wash the greens, slice the red onion, toast the almonds, hard-cook the eggs and prepare the salad dressing the day before. Cover and refrigerate each separately overnight. Do not toss the salad until just before serving.

- Roast the turkey breast, make the sauce and cook the bacon for the Hot Browns the day before (see page 134 for full details). Cover and refrigerate each separately overnight.

- Assemble the potato casserole the day before (see page 144 for full details).

Completing the Menu

- Fresh asparagus should be in season and would be an ideal accompaniment. To roast it, trim the stalks and arrange the asparagus in a single layer on a baking sheet. Drizzle with olive oil and season with salt and pepper. Roast in a 425°F (220°C) oven for 10 minutes or until tender-crisp.

- No Southern Derby party would be complete without mint juleps, lemonade and sweet iced tea.

Decorations

- Line the table with a pastel tablecloth and use your fine china and your best silver.

- Set vases full of fresh flowers on every available surface.

Mother's Day

Honor Mom's special day by gathering the entire family for a fantastic buffet at home, avoiding the crowds at the restaurants.

Hot Corn Dip (page 57)

Corn chips or tortilla chips

Coleslaw or fruit salad

New Orleans Spicy Barbecue Shrimp (page 136)

Crusty French bread

Strawberry Rhubarb Dessert (page 176)

Peach raspberry coolers

Countdown to the Party

- **4 to 5 hours ahead:** Start the Strawberry Rhubarb Dessert.
- **2 hours ahead:** Start the Hot Corn Dip.
- **1 hour ahead:** Start the New Orleans Spicy Barbecue Shrimp.
- **30 minutes before you want dessert:** Start the crust for the Strawberry Rhubarb Dessert.

Make Ahead Suggestion

- Assemble the dip the day before (see page 57 for full details).

Completing the Menu

- Set out a big bowl of corn chips or tortilla chips for dipping.
- In New Orleans, many restaurants serve their shrimp without side dishes, but Mom may appreciate a side of coleslaw or fruit salad. Either one is easy to toss together or pick up at the deli.
- Pick up the freshest crusty French bread you can find.

- To make peach raspberry coolers, combine equal parts white grape–peach fruit juice (prepared from frozen concentrate) and raspberry-flavored water. Serve over ice.

Decorations

- This shrimp is sometimes served outside, at picnic tables covered with newspaper. Weather permitting, follow that lead and keep it casual.
- Instead of newspaper, unroll brown or white paper and give everyone permanent markers so they can write notes of love and admiration for all that Mom does. Encourage the children to draw pictures for her. The table covering will be so special, she may want to roll it up before the food is served. Have a spare roll handy in case she does.
- Add a bouquet of flowers or a potted plant for her to keep.

Graduation Gathering

Graduations are the perfect time to host an open house so everyone can congratulate the graduate.

Vidalia Onion Dip (page 57)
Toasted baguette slices or thin wheat crackers
Tamale Meatballs (page 90)
Favorite Barbecue Ribs (page 80)
Vegetable crudités with dip
Fresh fruit
Cake pops
Lemonade, soft drinks

Countdown to the Party

- **7 to 9 hours ahead:** Start the Favorite Barbecue Ribs if you're cooking them on Low (if cooking on High, start $3\frac{1}{2}$ to $4\frac{1}{2}$ hours ahead), using a 4- to 6-quart slow cooker (see tip, page 80). Remember to broil them until crisp just before the party begins.

- **3 to 4 hours ahead:** Start the Tamale Meatballs if you're cooking them on Low (if cooking on High, start $1\frac{1}{2}$ to 2 hours ahead). Allow time for forming and baking them first if you haven't done this ahead.

- **2 to 3 hours ahead:** Start the Vidalia Onion Dip.

Make Ahead Suggestions

- Assemble the dip the day before (see page 57 for full details).

- Form and bake the meatballs the day before (see page 90 for full details).

- Many fresh vegetables and fruits can be cut ahead, but wait to wash, chop or peel fruits that discolor easily (such as bananas, apples or pears) and more delicate ones (such as berries) until just before the party. Dip chopped fruits that discolor in lemon juice to help keep them pretty.

Completing the Menu

- Set out a basket of toasted baguette slices or thin wheat crackers for dipping.

- Add color to the buffet with a tray of vegetable crudités surrounding a favorite dip, and another tray of fresh fruit.

- Finish the meal with cake pops baked in the Babycakes™ Cake Pop Maker, then coated in the colors of the graduate's high school, college or university. A gorgeous array of colorful cake pops serves as both a decoration and dessert.

- Set out pitchers of cold lemonade and ice water, and keep plenty of soft drinks on ice.

Decorations

- Decorate the table in school colors and sprinkle it with metallic cardboard stars to represent your graduate's "reach for the stars."

- Arrange pictures of the graduate around the room.

Bridal or Baby Shower

Whether it's for a bride-to-be or an expectant mom, a shower is a festive way to celebrate the blessings to come. This menu works beautifully for either occasion — just adjust the decorations.

Oyster Cracker Snacks (page 95)

Bacon-Wrapped Chicken Bites (page 79)

Vegetable crudités with dip

Fresh fruit

Creamy Caramel Fondue (page 167)

Apple slices, pound cake cubes, doughnut holes, marshmallows

Punch, lemonade, coffee

Countdown to the Party

- **2 hours ahead:** Start the Oyster Cracker Snacks.

- **1 to 2 hours ahead:** Start the Creamy Caramel Fondue.

- **1 hour ahead:** Start the Bacon-Wrapped Chicken Bites.

Make Ahead Suggestions

- For the chicken bites, pound the chicken, spread with cream cheese and roll in bacon early that day or the day before (see page 79 for full details).

- If serving cake cubes with the fondue, bake the cake the day before so it will be cool and ready to cut into cubes. Of course, you can always pick one up at a local bakery.

Completing the Menu

- Trays of fresh fruit and vegetables with a dip are gorgeous on the buffet table and will be appreciated by all.

- Set out an array of fondue dippers. If you prefer, you can choose another dessert fondue or dip (pages 164–170). Other dippers might include cubes of angel food cake or gingerbread cake, fresh berries or pretzels.

- Make up a bowl of festive punch (so pretty and refreshing), set out a pitcher of lemonade and brew a pot of coffee.

Decorations and Activities

- For a bridal shower, use the colors the bride plans to use in her wedding and set the table with old-fashioned dishes, antique glasses and simple flower arrangements. Cut out reproductions of old wedding photos from throughout history, frame them and set them on the buffet table and around the room. For fun, play a guessing game based on historical wedding trivia found on the Internet.

- For a twist on the usual pastel baby shower decorations, take inspiration from a nursery rhyme or fairy tale. Buy copies of a story collection that includes your choice and set them around the room, near baby rattles and booties. Use bright, festive colors for tablecloths and fresh flowers. For fun, ask guests trivia questions about the stories.

Father's Day

Keep Dad's day casual. Gather the family to enjoy a delicious meal and toss a ball around, play cards or head out fishing — whatever your dad enjoys!

Bacon Cheese Fondue (page 71)

Crusty bread cubes, sourdough, rye or pumpernickel bread cubes, pretzels, fresh vegetables

Beer-Braised Brats (page 130)

Split and toasted buns, mustard

Tangy Red Cabbage (page 157)

Brownies or chocolate layer cake

Ice-cold beer and root beer

Countdown to the Party

- **5 to 7 hours ahead:** Start the Tangy Red Cabbage if you're cooking it on Low (if cooking on High, start $2\frac{1}{2}$ to $3\frac{1}{2}$ hours ahead).

- **4 to 6 hours ahead:** Start the Beer-Braised Brats if you're cooking them on Low (if cooking on High, start 2 to 3 hours ahead).

- **30 minutes ahead:** Start the Bacon Cheese Fondue.

Make Ahead Suggestions

- For the fondue, shred the cheese, cook and crumble the bacon and slice the green onions the day before. Cover and refrigerate each separately overnight.

- For the cabbage dish, slice the cabbage and chop the onion the day before. Cover and refrigerate each separately overnight.

Completing the Menu

- Set out an array of dippers for the fondue.

- We like to serve the brats on toasted buns, garnished with mustard, but you know what your dad likes, so be sure to provide all his favorite accompaniments.

- Bake a batch of your dad's favorite brownies or pick up a decadent chocolate layer cake from a local bakery.

Decorations

- Let Dad's hobbies inspire the decorations and the gift. Include new golf balls, fishing lures or tickets to a sporting event in the centerpiece. Add a bouquet of helium balloons and presto — the table is festive and ready for Dad.

Get Out the Grill

Combine the ease of slow cooking with the fantastic flavor of grilled pork for an absolutely perfect dinner party. The Fig and Port Jam allows you to take the meat off the grill, slice it into medallions and keep it warm in the flavorful sauce.

Spinach, Bacon and Blue Cheese Dip (page 60)

Toasted baguette slices or crackers

Grilled Pork Tenderloin with Fig and Port Jam (page 126)

Corn on the cob, sliced tomatoes

Cheesecake Fondue (page 168)

Grilled fruit

Raspberry lemonade, local beers and wines,
wine coolers, bottled cocktails

Countdown to the Party

- **5 to 6 hours ahead:** Start the Fig and Port Jam.
- **2 hours ahead:** Start the Cheesecake Fondue.
- **1½ to 2 hours ahead:** Start the Spinach, Bacon and Blue Cheese Dip.
- **30 minutes ahead:** Start grilling the pork. Remember to allow time first for the barbecue grill to preheat.

Make Ahead Suggestions

- For the dip, chop the onion, mince the garlic, wash and trim the spinach, cook and crumble the bacon and toast the pecans the day before. Store each ingredient in a separate airtight container in the refrigerator overnight (the onion and garlic can be stored together).
- For the jam, chop the onions and figs the day before. Store them overnight in separate airtight containers in the refrigerator.

Completing the Menu

- Set out a basket of toasted baguette slices or crackers for dipping.
- Fresh produce, such as corn on the cob and sliced tomatoes, is all you need to complete the meal.
- The fondue is wonderful served with warm grilled fruit. Follow the tip on page 168, selecting a variety of firm but ripe fruits, such as peaches, pears and pineapple. Clear the table and refresh the drinks while grilling the fruit so it is hot off the grill when it's time for dessert.
- Use a large beverage tub to ice down bottles of beer, wine coolers and cocktails. Set out pitchers of raspberry lemonade on the table and serve over ice.

Decorations

- Serve this meal al fresco (outside). For casual elegance, select a brightly colored tablecloth and use your best dishes. Clip fresh flowers from your garden (or buy a variety of fresh flowers) and arrange loosely in a jar for a "wildflower" look.
- For ambiance, add twinkling outdoor Christmas lights in the trees nearby.

Family Reunion

Family reunions are a time to build memories and strengthen family ties. Kathy's family has discovered that the more often you have reunions, the closer you become and the more fun you have. With a menu this easy, we bet you'll volunteer to host more often.

Vegetable crudités with dip

Slow-Roasted Cola Pork (page 125)

Bacon Macaroni and Cheese (page 148)

Old-Fashioned Baked Beans (page 154)

Watermelon

Chocolate chip cookies or brownies

Iced tea, lemonade

Countdown to the Party

- **8 to 10 hours ahead:** Start the Slow-Roasted Cola Pork if you're cooking it on Low (if cooking on High, start 4 to 5 hours ahead).

- **4 to 6 hours ahead:** Start the Old-Fashioned Baked Beans if you're cooking them on Low (if cooking on High, start 2 to 3 hours ahead).

- **2 hours ahead:** Start the Bacon Macaroni and Cheese.

Make Ahead Suggestion

- Assemble the pork and the beans the day before (see pages 125 and 154 for full details).

Completing the Menu

- Add color to the buffet with a tray of vegetable crudités surrounding a favorite dip.

- Be sure to include your family's favorite foods, whether it's Grandma's peach cobbler or a special salad that reminds everyone of a loving aunt.

- Round out the menu with ice-cold watermelon or other fruits, cookies or brownies and plenty of iced tea and lemonades.

Decorations and Activities

- Use a colorful tablecloth and add an arrangement of fresh flowers to the table. Give the flowers to the oldest family member at the end of the day.

- Incorporate current and old family photos throughout the room — they are instant conversation starters.

- Make a large template of a family tree and display it so you can all fill it in together.

- Gather lots of board games and lawn games for the children, then plan an intergenerational game, like Family Feud or a family "Olympics."

Tailgate Party

Football season means tailgate time! Even if your party is in front of the television and not down at the arena, you can plan a festive, tasty gathering before the kickoff.

Buffalo Chicken Dip (page 66)
Tortilla chips or corn chips
Sticky Wings (page 77)
Hot-and-Spicy Chili (page 105)
Cookies or cupcakes
Beer, soft drinks

Countdown to the Party

- **6 to 8 hours ahead:** Start the Hot-and-Spicy Chili if you're cooking it on Low (if cooking on High, start 3 to 4 hours ahead). Allow time to cook the bacon and brown the beef and onion first if you haven't done this ahead.

- **4 to 5 hours ahead:** Start the Sticky Wings if you're cooking them on Low (if cooking on High, start 2 to $2\frac{1}{2}$ hours ahead). Remember to broil them until crisp just before the party begins.

- **2 to 3 hours ahead:** Start the Buffalo Chicken Dip.

Make Ahead Suggestions

- Assemble the dip and the chili the night before (see pages 66 and 105 for full details).

- Prepare the wings for cooking the night before (see page 77 for full details).

Completing the Menu

- Set out a big bowl of tortilla chips or corn chips for dipping.

- Add your favorite cookies or cupcakes, decorated in team colors or with football decorations.

- Keep plenty of beer and soft drinks on ice.

Decorations and Activities

- Team colors score big. Party stores sell paper goods in a variety of colors, and we bet you can find the colors you need without paying extra for the team logo. Display team pennants or flags nearby.

- Be sure to play the fight song!

- Before or after the game, encourage your guests to join you outdoors to toss a football around or play another outdoor game such as horseshoes, washers or beanbags.

Oktoberfest

Host a German-style fall festival, play polka music and dance the night away. The crisp, autumn air will make everyone hungry.

Cheese, sausage and fruit appetizer tray

Thinly sliced rye or pumpernickel bread

Kielbasa and Kraut (page 131)

German Potato Salad (page 145)

Apple strudel

Hot German Wine Punch (page 178)

German beers

Countdown to the Party

- **5 to 6 hours ahead:** Start the Kielbasa and Kraut if you're cooking it on Low (if cooking on High, start 3 to 3½ hours ahead).

- **4 to 6 hours ahead:** Start the Hot German Potato Salad if you're cooking it on Low (if cooking on High, start 2 to 3 hours ahead).

- **2 to 3 hours ahead:** Start the Hot German Wine Punch.

Make Ahead Suggestion

- Assemble the Kielbasa and Kraut the night before (see page 131 for full details).

- For the potato salad, parboil the potatoes, cook the bacon and prepare the onion mixture the night before (see page 145 for full details).

Completing the Menu

- Offer an assortment of cheeses, thinly sliced fully cooked sausages and ham, pickles and fresh fruits, such as grapes, apple slices and pear slices. A basket of thinly sliced rye or pumpernickel bread will round out the appetizer course.

- Purchase an apple strudel from your local bakery for a traditional dessert.

- Oktoberfest wouldn't be complete without a variety of cold German beers.

Decorations

- Unless it's too cold, plan an outdoor party and make the patio or deck look like a German beer garden, with twinkling lights and long rectangular tables.

- Use a color scheme of black, red and gold — the colors on the German flag — when setting the table. Add an arrangement of beer steins as a centerpiece.

Games Night

Set up the game tables and invite your friends over for a night of card or board games. With this menu, everyone will end up a winner.

Citrus-Glazed Wings (page 76)

Firehouse Meatballs (page 88)

Cuban Pork Sandwiches with Cilantro Mayonnaise (page 128)

Vegetable crudités with dip

Cupcakes

Soft drinks, iced tea, beer

Countdown to the Party

- **9 to 11 hours ahead:** Start the Cuban Pork if you're cooking it on Low (if cooking on High, start 5 to 6 hours ahead; if you've cooked the pork ahead, start reheating it 35 to 40 minutes ahead).

- **4 to 5 hours ahead:** Start the Citrus-Glazed Wings if you're cooking them on Low (if cooking on High, start 2 to $2\frac{1}{2}$ hours ahead). Remember to broil them until crisp just before the party begins.

- **3 to 4 hours ahead:** Start the Firehouse Meatballs if you're cooking them on Low (if cooking on High, start $1\frac{1}{2}$ to 2 hours ahead). Allow time for forming and browning them first if you haven't done this ahead.

Make Ahead Suggestions

- Prepare the wings for cooking the night before (see page 76 for full details).

- Form and brown the meatballs the day before (see page 88 for full details).

- For the sandwiches, cook the pork the day before (see page 128 for full details). The Cilantro Mayonnaise can also be prepared the day before.

Completing the Menu

- Offer a tray of vegetable crudités with a favorite dip.

- Bake up a batch of your favorite cupcakes.

- Make sure you have plenty of ice so the soft drinks, iced tea and beer stay cold all evening long.

Decorations

- Scatter game pieces — old, mismatched playing cards, Monopoly money, poker chips, score cards, Scrabble pieces, dice — around the buffet table.

- Follow the example of Roxanne's Bunko group and choose a theme — such as Hawaiian luau — or a color scheme for your table linens and paper goods. Give out prizes that reflect the theme.

- Set up tables and chairs as needed for the games. If you don't have card tables, use any other tables and place a large piece of felt on top of each to protect the surface.

Halloween

On Halloween night, there's often a chill in the air, so your guests are sure to appreciate a hot meal — but keep it easy so you can enjoy the fun. At Roxanne's house, chili dogs are a Halloween tradition.

Tortilla chips and salsa

All-Time Favorite Chili (page 104)

Hot Dogs (page 132)

Shredded cheese, chopped onions, sliced jalapeño peppers

Vegetable or fruit skewers

Our Favorite Hot Cider (page 180)

Countdown to the Party

- **6 to 8 hours ahead:** Start the All-Time Favorite Chili if you're cooking it on Low (if cooking on High, start 3 to 4 hours ahead). Allow time to cook brown the beef and onion first if you haven't done this ahead.
- **2 to 3 hours ahead:** Start Our Favorite Hot Cider.
- **1 to 2 hours ahead:** Start the Hot Dogs.

Make Ahead Suggestions

- Assemble the chili the night before (see page 104 for full details).
- Fix bowls of shredded cheese, chopped onions, sliced jalapeño peppers and other favorite chili toppings. Cover them tightly with plastic wrap and refrigerate overnight.

Completing the Menu

- Set out a basket of tortilla chips and a bowl of salsa so your guests have something to nibble on before dinner.
- Chili dogs are a meal in themselves, so you won't need to serve much else. But if you want to offer some fresh veggies or fruit, make them fun by threading pieces onto toothpicks and poking these skewers into a pumpkin, arranging them decoratively. (This would also make a colorful centerpiece.)

Decorations

- If you've already decorated for Halloween, you may not need other decorations — just rearrange what you have so it draws focus to the buffet table.
- Drape the buffet table in black and set a jack-o'-lantern or scary light-up character in the middle. Scatter plastic spiders around the table, drape cotton cobwebs off the edge and tie fabric ghosts to the ceiling above.
- Dim the lights and burn lots of candles. Play "Monster Mash" or a CD of spooky Halloween noises from a player positioned underneath the table.

Pasta Party

A pasta party offers your guests the opportunity to sample three different pasta sauces in one night and decide which one they like best.

Antipasto tray

Italian Salad (page 162)

Bolognese Sauce (page 112)

Eggplant Pasta Sauce (page 113)

Chicken and Mushroom Alfredo Sauce (page 114)

Pasta

Chianti, Pinot Grigio or Soave, San Pellegrino

Countdown to the Party

- **6 to 7 hours ahead:** Start the Eggplant Pasta Sauce if you're cooking it on Low (if cooking on High, start 3 to $3\frac{1}{2}$ hours ahead).
- **5 to 7 hours ahead:** Start the Bolognese Sauce if you're cooking it on Low (if cooking on High, start $2\frac{1}{2}$ to $3\frac{1}{2}$ hours ahead).
- **5 to 6 hours ahead:** Start the Chicken and Mushroom Alfredo Sauce if you're cooking it on Low (if cooking on High, start $2\frac{1}{2}$ to 3 hours ahead).

Make Ahead Suggestions

- For the salad, wash the greens, slice the onions, grate the Parmesan and prepare the dressing the day before. Cover and refrigerate each separately overnight. Bring the dressing to room temperature and whisk well before use. Do not toss the salad until just before serving.
- Assemble the Bolognese Sauce the day before (see page 112 for full details).

Completing the Menu

- To make an antipasto tray, arrange olives, marinated mushrooms or other prepared salad bar favorites, wedges of cheese, thin pieces of salami, roasted almonds and grapes on an attractive tray.

- For the pasta, we suggest a sturdy tubular pasta, such as rigatoni or ziti, or a fun shape, such as farfalle (bow ties). Long pastas, such as spaghetti and fettuccini, taste great with these sauces but must be very freshly cooked when served so they don't stick together; rigatoni and ziti are more forgiving. Slightly undercook the pasta, then keep it in a colander, ready to dip into boiling water to reheat and moisten it as you serve.
- Offer classic Italian wines — both a red, such as Chianti, and a white, such as Pinot Grigio or Soave. Set out bottles of San Pellegrino (an Italian sparkling mineral water) for those who prefer a nonalcoholic beverage.

Decorations

- Pasta comes in so many different shapes and colors, so use it to create a centerpiece and to make the buffet table look inviting. Position the slow cooker, the antipasto tray and the salad on the table, then fill in gaps with interesting arrangements of dried pasta, colorful fresh eggplants, zucchini, red or green bell peppers, lemons or grapes.

Thanksgiving

Host the annual feast with ease. The Triple Slow Cooker erases all worries about last-minute preparations.

Winter Salad (page 161)

Roast turkey

Savory Sage Bread Dressing (page 142)

Mashed Potatoes (page 143)

Roasted Sweet Potatoes (page 146)

Hot rolls with butter

Pumpkin pie and/or pecan pie

Cranberry spritzers

Countdown to the Party

- **5 to 6 hours ahead:** Start the Savory Sage Bread Dressing if you're cooking it on Low (if cooking on High, start $2\frac{1}{2}$ to 3 hours ahead).
- **4 to 5 hours ahead:** Start the Roasted Sweet Potatoes.
- **2 to 3 hours ahead:** Start cooking the Mashed Potatoes. Allow time to chop and boil the potatoes first.

Make Ahead Suggestions

- For the salad, wash the greens, cook and crumble the bacon, toast the walnuts and prepare the salad dressing the day before. Cover and refrigerate each separately overnight. Bring the dressing to room temperature and whisk well before use. Do not toss the salad until just before serving.
- For the dressing, bake the bread cubes the day before. Let stand at room temperature overnight so they are very dry the next day. Chop the celery and onion the night before and refrigerate in an airtight container.
- Assemble the Mashed Potatoes the night before (see page 143 for full details). You'll need to remove them from the refrigerator $3\frac{1}{2}$ to $4\frac{1}{2}$ hours ahead of the party and start cooking them 3 to 4 hours ahead.

Completing the Menu

- Roast the turkey as you normally would.
- If you prefer, you could prepare the Classic Green Bean Casserole (page 156) instead of one of the other sides. Allow 4 to 6 hours for it to cook.
- Set out a basket of hot rolls and a dish of butter.
- Purchase a pumpkin pie and/or a pecan pie from your local bakery to serve for dessert.
- To make cranberry spritzers, combine cranberry juice cocktail and lemon-lime soda. Freeze fresh cranberries in the ice cubes and garnish each glass with an orange slice.

Decorations

- Natural fall decorations make a beautiful table with very little work. Nestle small, colorful pumpkins, squash and gourds around the slow cooker and scatter fall leaves around the table.
- Fill two shallow serving platters with whole nuts and nestle pillar candles of various heights among the nuts. Place one platter on either side of the slow cooker.

Christmas Evening

Holiday evenings are magical. Whether your family and friends are gathering for Christmas Eve or after caroling or sledding, the food provides a luscious backdrop for a fun, memorable evening.

Mushroom and Caramelized Onion Bruschetta (page 92)

Zesty Holiday Cocktail Sausages (page 82)

Sliced ham

Vegetable crudités with dip

Christmas cookies

Holiday Cranberry Punch (page 179)

Countdown to the Party

- **2 to 4 hours ahead:** Start the Zesty Holiday Cocktail Sausages if you're cooking them on Low (if cooking on High, start 1 to 2 hours ahead).
- **2 to 3 hours ahead:** Start the Holiday Cranberry Punch.
- **1 to 2 hours ahead:** Start the Mushroom and Caramelized Onion Bruschetta. Allow time to thinly slice and sauté the mushrooms first.

Make Ahead Suggestions

- Assemble the sausages the night before (see page 82 for full details).
- For the bruschetta, prepare the caramelized onions, following the recipe on page 158, up to 3 days ahead if storing in the refrigerator or up to 6 months ahead if storing in the freezer. If frozen, let thaw overnight.

Completing the Menu

- This is the perfect time to serve a spiral ham.
- Add color to the buffet with a tray of vegetable crudités. Pick up a chilled vegetable dip at the store, or prepare your favorite recipe. To make a festive serving container, hollow out a red or green bell pepper, fill it with the dip and place it in the center of the vegetable tray.
- Arrange a selection of your favorite holiday cookies on a platter.

Decorations

- Begin with a festive tablecloth. Plan where the slow cooker and other dishes will sit, then place holiday candles in between.
- Adorn the buffet table with pretty glass jars filled with holiday candies. Nestle evergreen boughs wherever there's empty space. Accent some boughs with holly, but keep holly away from the front of the table, where reaching hands might brush against it — those edges are sharp!

Ski Trip

After a day on the slopes, everyone will be hungry, but no one wants to spend hours in the kitchen and miss out on all the fun. No problem — with this easy menu, the food will be ready when you are.

Beer and Cheese Soup (page 100)

Steak Fajita Chili (page 107)

Sour cream, guacamole, shredded cheese, salsa

Hot Cocoa for a Crowd (page 181)

Marshmallows, whipped cream, peppermint sticks, liqueurs

Countdown to the Party

- **$7\frac{1}{2}$ to 10 hours ahead:** Start the Beer and Cheese Soup if you're cooking it on Low (if cooking on High, start 4 to $5\frac{1}{2}$ hours ahead).

- **6 to 8 hours ahead:** Start the Steak Fajita Chili if you're cooking it on Low (if cooking on High, start 3 to 4 hours ahead). Allow time to brown the steak first if you haven't done this ahead.

- **2 to 3 hours ahead:** Start the Hot Cocoa for a Crowd.

- **30 to 60 minutes ahead:** Add the remaining ingredients to the Beer and Cheese Soup.

Make Ahead Suggestions

- For the soup, chop the onion, carrot, celery and red pepper the night before and refrigerate in an airtight container. Shred the cheese, cook and crumble the bacon and slice the green onions. Cover and refrigerate each separately overnight.

- Assemble the chili the night before (see page 107 for full details).

Completing the Menu

- The chili can be served in bowls with crushed tortilla chips on top, or it can be spooned into warm flour tortillas and rolled up. You may want to set out some of each so that everyone can make their own decision.

- Set out an array of condiments for the chili. Other toppings might include sliced jalapeño peppers, sliced green onions or pico de gallo.

- Make the cocoa even more fun by setting out bowls of marshmallows and whipped cream. Add peppermint sticks for stirring. For an adult gathering, offer an array of liqueurs, such as crème de cacao, peppermint schnapps, crème de menthe or Kahlúa, to spike it up.

Decorations and Activities

- All you need is a roaring fire in the fireplace.

- Challenge each guest to wear their brightest, ugliest, funniest, woolliest, warmest or prettiest sweater. Award prizes.

Part 2

Recipes for the Triple Slow Cooker

Dips and Cheese Fondues

Queso Dip

What separates this queso dip from the thousands of others? White American cheese. Enough said! Serve with tortilla chips or fresh vegetables, such as broccoli florets, grape tomatoes and celery sticks.

Tip

White American cheese is not typically available in packages, so purchase it at the deli department in the grocery store.

Make Ahead

Prepare dip through step 2, cover and refrigerate overnight. Cook as directed.

	Nonstick baking spray	
1 tbsp	vegetable oil	15 mL
½ cup	finely diced onion	125 mL
1	large jalapeño pepper, seeded and finely chopped	1
1 lb	white American cheese or white processed cheese slices, cut into 1-inch (2.5 cm) cubes	500 g
8 oz	pepper Jack cheese, cut into 1-inch (2.5 cm) cubes	250 g
¾ cup	milk	175 mL
3 tbsp	salsa verde	45 mL
2	plum (Roma) tomatoes, seeded and diced	2
⅓ cup	chopped fresh cilantro	75 mL

1. Spray one slow cooker stoneware with baking spray.

2. In a small skillet, heat oil over medium-high heat. Add onion and cook, stirring often, for about 3 minutes or until tender. Transfer to prepared stoneware. Stir in jalapeño, American cheese, pepper Jack cheese, milk and salsa verde.

3. Cover and cook on High for 2 to 3 hours, stirring once every hour, until melted and smooth. Turn to Warm for serving. Sprinkle with diced tomatoes and cilantro just before serving.

Hot Corn Dip

Makes about 5 cups (1.25 L)

This delightfully different dip is captivating. Serve with corn chips or tortilla chips.

Tip

Canned corn with red and green bell peppers (such as Mexicorn) adds flavor and color, but if you prefer, you can substitute plain canned whole-kernel corn.

Make Ahead

Prepare dip through step 2, cover and refrigerate overnight. Cook as directed.

	Nonstick baking spray	
2	cans (each 11 oz or 341 mL) whole-kernel corn with red and green bell peppers, drained	2
1	can (4 oz/113 mL) chopped mild green chiles	1
1/4 cup	drained chopped pickled jalapeños	60 mL
2 cups	shredded Cheddar-Jack cheese	500 mL
3/4 cup	freshly grated Parmesan cheese	175 mL
1 cup	mayonnaise	250 mL

1. Spray one slow cooker stoneware with baking spray.

2. In a medium bowl, combine corn, green chiles and jalapeños. Stir in Cheddar-Jack, Parmesan and mayonnaise. Transfer to prepared stoneware.

3. Cover and cook on High for $1\frac{1}{2}$ to 2 hours, stirring once every hour, until cheese is melted. Turn to Warm for serving.

Vidalia Onion Dip

Makes about 4 cups (1 L)

Roxanne's sister-in-law, Susie Wyss, shared this recipe with Roxanne several years ago, and it has become a staple at family get-togethers and parties. Serve with toasted baguette slices or thin wheat crackers.

Make Ahead

Prepare dip through step 2, cover and refrigerate overnight. Cook as directed.

	Nonstick baking spray	
2 cups	finely chopped Vidalia onions	500 mL
2 cups	shredded Swiss cheese	500 mL
1 2/3 cups	mayonnaise	400 mL
1/4 tsp	garlic salt	1 mL

1. Spray one slow cooker stoneware with baking spray.

2. In a medium bowl, stir together onions, cheese, mayonnaise and garlic salt until well combined. Transfer to prepared stoneware.

3. Cover and cook on High for 2 to 3 hours, stirring once every hour, until melted and smooth. Turn to Warm for serving.

Cheesy Black-Eyed Pea Dip

Makes about 4½ cups (1.125 L)

Serving black-eyed pea dip on New Year's Eve is a Southern tradition that promises a great new year. Make it your family's new tradition, too. Serve with tortilla chips or corn chips.

Tip

If you prefer, you can use 1 large fresh jalapeño pepper, seeded and chopped, instead of the pickled jalapeño.

Make Ahead

Prepare dip through step 3, cover and refrigerate overnight. Cook as directed.

	Nonstick baking spray	
¼ cup	unsalted butter	60 mL
½ cup	chopped onion	125 mL
2	cloves garlic, minced	2
2	cans (each 14 to 19 oz/398 to 540 mL) black-eyed peas, drained and rinsed	2
8 oz	cream cheese, softened and cut into ½-inch (1 cm) cubes	250 g
2 cups	shredded sharp (old) Cheddar cheese	500 mL
2 tbsp	drained pickled jalapeño slices, chopped	30 mL
1	can (4 oz/113 g) chopped mild green chiles	1
	Salt and freshly ground black pepper	

1. Spray one slow cooker stoneware with baking spray.

2. In a small skillet, melt butter over medium-high heat. Add onion and garlic; cook, stirring often, for about 3 minutes or until onion is tender. Transfer to prepared stoneware.

3. Pour half the black-eyed peas into a bowl. Using a potato masher or the tines of a fork, mash until fairly smooth. Transfer to the slow cooker stoneware. Stir in the remaining peas, cream cheese, Cheddar, jalapeños and green chiles. Season to taste with salt and pepper.

4. Cover and cook on High for 2 to 3 hours, stirring once every hour, until cheese is melted and dip is hot. Turn to Warm for serving.

Tex-Mex Spinach Dip

Makes about 4 cups (1 L)

This all-time favorite is so simple, yet it tastes just like the dip at the best Mexican restaurants. Serve with tortilla chips or fresh vegetables.

Tips

Be sure to squeeze the spinach dry before combining it with the other ingredients.

Shredded Cheddar, Cheddar-Jack, Monterey Jack or Mexican cheese blend can all be used in place of the Colby-Jack cheese.

If you prefer a thinner dip, stir in an additional 1/4 to 1/2 cup (60 to 125 mL) salsa during the last 15 minutes of cooking.

Make Ahead

Prepare dip through step 3, cover and refrigerate overnight. Cook as directed.

1	package (10 oz/300 g) frozen chopped spinach	1
	Nonstick baking spray	
1	can (10 oz/284 mL) diced tomatoes and green chiles, with juice	1
8 oz	cream cheese, softened and cut into 1/2-inch (1 cm) cubes	250 g
2 cups	shredded Colby-Jack cheese	500 mL
1/4 cup	salsa	60 mL

1. Thaw spinach and drain well, squeezing between paper towels until dry.
2. Spray one slow cooker stoneware with baking spray.
3. In a large bowl, combine spinach, tomatoes and chiles with juice, cream cheese, Colby-Jack and salsa. Transfer to prepared stoneware.
4. Cover and cook on High for 1 hour, stirring occasionally, until cheese is melted and dip is hot. Turn to Warm for serving.

Spinach, Bacon and Blue Cheese Dip

Makes about 4 cups (1 L)

Here, the popular flavors of bacon, spinach and blue cheese are combined into one scrumptious dip. Serve with toasted baguette slices or crackers.

Tip

Toasting pecans intensifies their flavor. Spread chopped pecans in a single layer on a baking sheet. Bake at 350°F (180°C) for 5 to 7 minutes or until lightly browned. Let cool.

	Nonstick baking spray	
2 tbsp	unsalted butter	30 mL
1/3 cup	chopped onion	75 mL
2	cloves garlic, minced	2
1	package (6 oz/175 g) fresh spinach (about 6 cups/1.5 L lightly packed), trimmed	1
10	slices bacon, cooked crisp and crumbled	10
1 lb	cream cheese, softened and cut into 1/2-inch (1 cm) cubes	500 g
1/2 cup	crumbled blue cheese	125 mL
1/2 cup	sour cream	125 mL
1/2 cup	chopped pecans, toasted (see tip, at left)	125 mL

1. Spray one slow cooker stoneware with baking spray.

2. In a medium skillet, melt butter over medium-high heat. Add onion and garlic; cook, stirring often, for about 3 minutes or until onion is tender. Add spinach and cook, stirring often, for 3 to 4 minutes or until wilted. Transfer to prepared stoneware. Stir in bacon, cream cheese, blue cheese and sour cream.

3. Cover and cook on High for $1\frac{1}{2}$ to 2 hours, stirring occasionally, until cheese is melted and dip is hot. Turn to Warm for serving. Sprinkle with pecans just before serving.

Artichoke and Spinach Dip

Makes about 6 cups (1.5 L)

No need to go to a restaurant for this favorite dip — now you can make your own any time. Serve with toasted baguette slices, tortilla chips or corn chips.

Tip

If you like, you can top this dip with ½ cup (125 mL) toasted chopped pecans just before serving.

Make Ahead

Prepare dip through step 3, cover and refrigerate overnight. Cook as directed.

	Nonstick baking spray	
2 tbsp	unsalted butter	30 mL
1	onion, chopped	1
3	cloves garlic, minced	3
1	package (6 oz/175 g) fresh spinach (about 6 cups/1.5 L lightly packed), trimmed	1
1	can (14 oz/398 mL) artichoke hearts, drained and chopped	1
8 oz	cream cheese, softened and cut into ½-inch (1 cm) cubes	250 g
2 cups	shredded Cheddar or Colby-Jack cheese	500 mL
¾ cup	freshly grated Parmesan cheese	175 mL
½ cup	mayonnaise	125 mL

1. Spray one slow cooker stoneware with baking spray.

2. In a medium skillet, melt butter over medium-high heat. Add onion and garlic; cook, stirring often, for about 3 minutes or until onion is tender. Add spinach and cook, stirring often, for 3 to 4 minutes or until wilted.

3. Pour spinach mixture into a large bowl. Stir in artichoke hearts, cream cheese, Cheddar, Parmesan and mayonnaise. Transfer to prepared stoneware.

4. Cover and cook on High for 1 to 2 hours, stirring once every hour, until cheese is melted and dip is hot. Turn to Warm for serving.

Hearts of Palm Dip

Makes about 3 cups (750 mL)

This elegant dip is perfect for any special gathering. If you have never eaten hearts of palm, they are a treat worth trying. They may remind you of artichokes, but they have a captivating texture and flavor that are all their own. Serve this dip with toasted baguette slices or crackers.

Tip

Hearts of palm are the nutritious inner stems of the *Sabal palmetto*, a palm tree that has been named the state tree of Florida. Considered a poor man's food during the 1920s and '30s, they have risen in status to a delicacy prized for its flavor. The long, slender, ivory-colored stalks resemble smooth asparagus stems, without the texture and tips. Hearts of palm are found canned at well-stocked supermarkets.

Make Ahead

Prepare dip through step 2, cover and refrigerate overnight. Cook as directed.

	Nonstick baking spray	
2	green onions, finely chopped	2
1	can (14 oz/398 mL) hearts of palm, drained and finely diced	1
1 cup	shredded mozzarella cheese	250 mL
1/2 cup	freshly grated Parmesan cheese	125 mL
1/4 tsp	garlic powder	1 mL
3/4 cup	mayonnaise	175 mL
1/4 cup	sour cream	60 mL

1. Spray one slow cooker stoneware with baking spray.

2. In a bowl, combine green onions, hearts of palm, mozzarella cheese, Parmesan, garlic powder, mayonnaise and sour cream. Transfer to prepared stoneware.

3. Cover and cook on High for 1 hour, stirring after 30 minutes, until cheese is melted and dip is hot. Turn to Warm for serving.

Gruyère and Wild Rice Dip

Makes about 4½ cups (1.125 L)

When Roxanne's husband, Bob Bateman, treated her to a weekend getaway at a beautiful bed and breakfast in Kansas City, they were served a wonderful wild rice and Gruyère dip. This adaptation of that recipe is perfect for entertaining. Serve with toasted baguette slices or crackers.

Tips

Gruyère cheese is a flavorful Swiss cheese. If it's not available, substitute another good-quality Swiss cheese.

One-half to ⅔ cup (125 to 150 mL) of uncooked wild rice will make about 2 cups (500 mL) cooked. Follow package directions, or simmer in about 2 cups (500 mL) salted water for 45 minutes or until tender. Drain and stir into dip. Any leftover cooked wild rice is a great addition to a soup or stew.

Make Ahead

Prepare dip through step 2, cover and refrigerate for up to 6 hours. Cook as directed.

	Nonstick baking spray	
2 tbsp	unsalted butter	30 mL
½ cup	chopped onion	125 mL
2	cloves garlic, minced	2
1 lb	cream cheese, softened and cut into ½-inch (1 cm) cubes	500 g
2 cups	shredded Gruyère cheese	500 mL
2 cups	cooked wild rice (see tip, at left)	500 mL
1 tbsp	dried tarragon	15 mL
½ cup	sour cream	125 mL
	Salt and freshly ground black pepper	

1. Spray one slow cooker stoneware with baking spray.

2. In a small skillet, melt butter over medium-high heat. Add onion and garlic; cook, stirring often, for about 3 minutes or until onion is tender. Transfer to prepared stoneware. Stir in cream cheese, Gruyère, wild rice, tarragon and sour cream. Season to taste with salt and pepper.

3. Cover and cook on High for 1 hour, stirring after 30 minutes, until cheese is melted and dip is hot. Turn to Warm for serving.

Crab Rangoon Dip

Makes about 3 cups (750 mL)

This rich dip is wonderful with corn chips or tortilla chips as dippers, but for an extra-special treat, deep-fry wonton wrappers until crisp (see box, at right) — you will think you are eating crab Rangoon at the finest restaurant.

Tip

If you prefer a thinner dip, stir in 2 to 3 tbsp (30 to 45 mL) half-and-half (10%) cream or milk during the last 15 minutes of cooking.

Make Ahead

Prepare dip through step 2, cover and refrigerate overnight. Be sure to cover it tightly, or open and stir in the canned crab just before cooking. Cook as directed.

	Nonstick baking spray	
1	can (6 oz/175 g) crabmeat, drained	1
1 tsp	garlic powder	5 mL
1/2 tsp	hot pepper sauce	2 mL
8 oz	cream cheese, softened and cut into 1/2-inch (1 cm) cubes	250 g
1/4 cup	unsalted butter, cut into pieces	60 mL
2 tsp	Worcestershire sauce	10 mL

1. Spray one slow cooker stoneware with baking spray.

2. In a medium bowl, combine crabmeat, garlic powder, hot pepper sauce, cream cheese, butter and Worcestershire sauce. Transfer to prepared stoneware.

3. Cover and cook on High for 1 hour, stirring after 30 minutes, until cheese is melted and dip is hot. Turn to Warm for serving.

Fried Wonton Wrappers

To deep-fry wonton wrappers, preheat a deep fryer filled with vegetable oil to 350°F (180°C) according to the manufacturer's directions. Cut each wonton wrapper into three strips. Fry wonton strips, in batches as necessary, for 30 to 60 seconds or just until golden. Remove with a slotted spoon and drain on a plate lined with paper towels. If preparing ahead, let cool completely, then store between layers of paper towels in an airtight container at room temperature for up to 1 day. When ready to serve, arrange on a baking sheet and bake at 375°F (190°C) for 10 to 15 minutes or until warm and crisp.

Chicken Enchilada Dip

**Makes about
6 cups (1.5 L)**

This recipe was created
by Roxanne's niece,
Libby Wyss. After she
served it at a family
gathering, everyone
was clamoring for the
recipe. Thanks, Libby!
Serve with tortilla chips.

Tips

You can substitute
leftover cooked chicken for
the canned chicken; you'll
need about 2 cups (500 mL)
diced.

If you have any leftover dip,
it makes a great filling for a
flour tortilla.

Make Ahead

Prepare dip through step 2,
cover and refrigerate
overnight. Cook as directed.

	Nonstick baking spray	
2	cans (each 9.75 oz/290 g) chicken breast, drained	2
1	can (10 oz/284 mL) condensed cream of chicken soup	1
1	can (4 oz/113 mL) chopped mild green chiles	1
1 cup	shredded Cheddar cheese	250 mL
1 cup	sour cream	250 mL
¼ cup	salsa verde	60 mL
	Chopped green onions	

1. Spray one slow cooker stoneware with baking spray.

2. In a medium bowl, combine chicken, cream of chicken soup, green chiles, Cheddar, sour cream and salsa verde. Transfer to prepared stoneware.

3. Cover and cook on High for 2 to 3 hours, stirring once every hour, until melted and smooth. Turn to Warm for serving. Sprinkle with green onions just before serving.

Buffalo Chicken Dip

**Makes about
5 cups (1.25 L)**

The flavors of Buffalo wings — chicken, ranch dressing, blue cheese and hot wing sauce — are captured in this fantastic dip. Serve with tortilla chips and celery sticks.

Tip

In place of the cooked chicken, you can use canned chicken. Three cans (each 9.75 oz/290 g), drained, will equal about 3 cups (750 mL).

Make Ahead

Prepare dip through step 2, cover and refrigerate overnight. Cook as directed.

	Nonstick baking spray	
3 cups	finely chopped rotisserie or grilled chicken	750 mL
8 oz	cream cheese, softened and cut into ½-inch (1 cm) cubes	250 g
¾ cup	shredded mozzarella cheese	175 mL
½ cup	crumbled blue cheese	125 mL
½ cup	ranch dressing	125 mL
½ cup	hot wing sauce	125 mL
2 tbsp	unsalted butter, cut into pieces	30 mL

1. Spray one slow cooker stoneware with baking spray.

2. In a medium bowl, combine chicken, cream cheese, mozzarella, blue cheese, ranch dressing, wing sauce and butter. Transfer to prepared stoneware.

3. Cover and cook on High for 2 to 3 hours, stirring once every hour, until melted and smooth. Turn to Warm for serving.

Pizza Dip

Makes about 4 cups (1 L)

This dip tastes just like a warm and wonderful pepperoni pizza. Serve with bread sticks, French bread cubes or wedges of warm pita bread.

Tip

For instant pizza, spread about 1½ cups (375 mL) cooked or leftover Pizza Dip over a 12-inch (30 cm) pizza crust. Top with additional shredded cheese. Bake at 425°F (220°C) for 10 to 15 minutes or until crust is golden and cheese is melted.

Make Ahead

Prepare dip through step 2, cover and refrigerate overnight. Cook as directed.

	Nonstick baking spray	
2 tbsp	olive oil	30 mL
1	green bell pepper, chopped	1
¾ cup	chopped onion	175 mL
1 cup	chopped mushrooms	250 mL
2	cloves garlic, minced	2
1	jar (24 oz/680 mL) spaghetti sauce	1
½ cup	chopped pepperoni	125 mL
½ tsp	dried oregano	2 mL
½ cup	shredded mozzarella cheese or Italian cheese blend	125 mL

1. Spray one slow cooker stoneware with baking spray.

2. In a medium skillet, heat oil over medium-high heat. Add green pepper and onion; cook, stirring often, for 2 to 3 minutes or until starting to soften. Stir in mushrooms and garlic; cook, stirring often, for 4 to 5 minutes or until vegetables are tender. Transfer to prepared stoneware. Stir in spaghetti sauce, pepperoni and oregano.

3. Cover and cook on Low for 2 to 4 hours or on High for 1 hour, until hot. Turn to Warm for serving. Stir in mozzarella just before serving.

Bacon Cheeseburger Dip

Makes about 6 cups (1.5 L)

Bacon, beef and cheese — what's not to love? Serve with tortilla chips or corn chips.

Tips

Bacon plays a dominant role in this dip, so you can create slightly different flavors by experimenting with different brands and types of bacon. Butcher shops and meat markets often specialize in a distinctive smoke flavor, such as applewood, or flavor the bacon with garlic or black pepper.

If you like spicy food, stir in hot pepper sauce to taste, adding a few drops at a time.

	Nonstick baking spray	
1 lb	sliced bacon	500 g
8 oz	lean ground beef	250 g
1	can (14 oz/398 mL) diced tomatoes, with juice	1
1	can (10 oz/284 mL) diced tomatoes and green chiles, with juice	1
8 oz	cream cheese, softened and cut into 1/2-inch (1 cm) cubes	250 g
3 cups	shredded Cheddar cheese, divided	750 mL
1/4 cup	ketchup	60 mL
2 tbsp	spicy mustard	30 mL

1. Spray one slow cooker stoneware with baking spray.

2. In a large skillet, cook bacon over medium heat, in batches as necessary, until crisp. Transfer bacon to a plate lined with paper towels to drain. Drain off all but 2 tbsp (30 mL) fat from the pan.

3. Add beef to the fat remaining in the pan and cook, breaking up beef with a spoon, for 5 to 6 minutes or until browned. Drain off fat. Transfer to prepared stoneware. Stir in tomatoes with juice, tomatoes and green chiles with juice, cream cheese, 2 cups (500 mL) of the Cheddar, ketchup and mustard.

4. Crumble bacon. Reserve 1/4 cup (60 mL) of the bacon, cover and refrigerate. Stir the remaining bacon into dip.

5. Cover and cook on High for 2 hours, stirring occasionally, until cheese is melted. Turn to Low and sprinkle with the remaining Cheddar and the reserved bacon. Cover and cook on Low for 30 minutes. Turn to Warm for serving.

Beef and Cream Cheese Dip

Makes about 3 cups (750 mL)

This dip has withstood the test of time and it is as warm and comforting today as it was when first created many years ago. Serve with toasted baguette slices or French bread cubes.

Tips

Look for shelf-stable packages of thinly sliced or chipped dried beef. If this product is not available in your area, substitute chopped thinly sliced deli roast beef or ham.

If desired, thin the dip with a little more milk or some white wine during the last 15 minutes of cooking.

You can enliven this dip with the trendy flavor of chipotle pepper by stirring in a chopped canned chipotle pepper in adobo sauce with the beef.

	Nonstick baking spray	
1 lb	cream cheese, softened and cut into $\frac{1}{2}$-inch (1 cm) cubes	500 g
1 cup	milk	250 mL
1	package (2$\frac{1}{2}$ oz/75 g) sliced dried beef (see tip, at left), finely chopped	1
2	cloves garlic, minced	2
$\frac{1}{4}$ cup	finely chopped onion	60 mL
2 tsp	dry mustard	10 mL
	Freshly ground black pepper	

1. Spray one slow cooker stoneware with baking spray.

2. In prepared stoneware, combine cream cheese and milk, stirring well.

3. Cover and cook on Low for 1 to 2 hours, stirring occasionally, until cheese is melted. Stir in beef, garlic, onion, mustard and pepper to taste. Cover and cook on Low for 30 minutes or until warmed through. Turn to Warm for serving.

Classic Cheese Fondue

Makes about 3 cups (750 mL)

Old-world flavors come together in this classic fondue that's easy to make and easy to serve. Serve with crusty French bread cubes or crusty rolls and/or fresh vegetables, such as broccoli florets, carrot sticks or roasted new potatoes.

Tips

Other vegetables that are especially good with cheese fondue are mushrooms, cherry tomatoes, cauliflower florets and red bell pepper strips.

Gruyère cheese is a flavorful Swiss cheese. If it's not available, substitute another good-quality Swiss cheese.

1	clove garlic, cut in half	1
1 cup	dry white wine (such as Sauvignon Blanc)	250 mL
12 oz	Gruyère cheese, shredded	375 g
6 oz	fontina cheese, shredded	175 g
2 tbsp	all-purpose flour	30 mL
Pinch	ground nutmeg	Pinch

1. Rub the walls of one slow cooker stoneware with garlic. Discard garlic. Pour wine into stoneware. Microwave on High for 2 to 3 minutes or until wine is steaming hot.

2. Place stoneware in slow cooker and turn to High. In a bowl, toss Gruyère and fontina cheese with flour. Stirring constantly, gradually add cheese mixture to wine, adding cheese by the handful and stirring well after each addition.

3. Cover and cook on High for 30 minutes, stirring often, until hot and melted. Sprinkle with nutmeg. Turn to Warm for serving.

Bacon Cheese Fondue

**Makes about
3 cups (750 mL)**

This fondue is as
welcome at an evening
reception as it is at a
casual gathering to
watch the big game.
Serve with crusty
bread cubes, rye or
pumpernickel bread
cubes, pretzels, fresh
vegetables and/or
fully cooked smoked
sausage slices or
cocktail sausages.

Tips

You can use any type of
beer in this recipe. A lager is
known for a crisp, dry flavor,
while a dark stout or ale
will give the fondue a more
robust flavor.

If you choose pretzels as
one of your dippers, you
might select crisp pretzel
sticks or larger soft pretzels,
cut into bite-size pieces. Soft
pretzel pieces are especially
good warm.

1	clove garlic, halved	1
1 cup	beer, at room temperature	250 mL
12 oz	Cheddar cheese, shredded	375 g
6 oz	Swiss cheese, shredded	175 g
2 tbsp	all-purpose flour	30 mL
1 tsp	Worcestershire sauce	5 mL
2 to 3	drops hot pepper sauce	2 to 3
4	slices bacon, cooked crisp and crumbled	4
2	green onions, sliced	2

1. Rub the walls of one slow cooker stoneware with garlic. Discard garlic. Pour beer into stoneware. Microwave on High for 2 to 3 minutes or until beer is steaming hot.

2. Place stoneware in slow cooker and turn to High. In a bowl, toss Cheddar and Swiss cheese with flour. Stirring constantly, gradually add cheese mixture to beer, adding cheese by the handful and stirring well after each addition. Stir in Worcestershire sauce and hot pepper sauce.

3. Cover and cook on High for 30 minutes, stirring often, until hot and melted. Stir in bacon and green onions. Turn to Warm for serving.

Fondue Italiano

Makes about 4 cups (1 L)

If you love classic Italian cuisine, you'll love this fondue. Serve with hot bread sticks, Italian bread cubes, small mushroom caps and/or fully cooked smoked Italian sausage slices.

Tip

For a thinner fondue, stir in ¼ cup (60 mL) red wine, beef broth or additional tomato juice during the last 15 minutes of cooking.

Make Ahead

Prepare fondue through step 2, cover and refrigerate overnight. Cook as directed.

	Nonstick baking spray	
2 tbsp	olive oil	30 mL
½ cup	finely chopped onion	125 mL
¼ cup	finely chopped green bell pepper	60 mL
3	cloves garlic, minced	3
2	cans (each 8 oz/227 mL) tomato sauce	2
1	can (6 oz/170 mL) tomato paste	1
1½ cups	tomato juice	375 mL
1½ tsp	dried Italian seasoning	7 mL
	Salt and freshly ground black pepper	
1 cup	shredded mozzarella cheese	250 mL

1. Spray one slow cooker stoneware with baking spray.

2. In a medium saucepan, heat oil over medium-high heat. Add onion, green pepper and garlic; cook, stirring often, for 3 to 4 minutes or until tender-crisp. Transfer to prepared stoneware. Stir in tomato sauce, tomato paste, tomato juice and Italian seasoning.

3. Cover and cook on High for 1 hour or until hot. Turn to Low and stir in mozzarella. Cover and cook on Low for 30 minutes or until melted. Turn to Warm for serving.

Appetizers and Snacks

Garlic Mushrooms

We enjoy tapas — Spain's take on the appetizer — because we can order several small plates of food to share and sample a variety of different dishes. These garlicky mushrooms were inspired by various tapas dishes we have enjoyed.

Tip

Look for tomato paste in a tube instead of a can when you need just a small amount. Once opened, store the tube in the refrigerator and use within about 45 days.

3 tbsp	olive oil	45 mL
1½ lbs	mushrooms	750 g
4	cloves garlic, minced	4
1 tsp	dried Italian seasoning	5 mL
½ tsp	salt	2 mL
¼ tsp	freshly ground black pepper	1 mL
⅛ to ¼ tsp	hot pepper flakes	0.5 to 1 mL
3 tbsp	white wine	45 mL
1 tbsp	tomato paste	15 mL
1 tbsp	minced fresh oregano or flat-leaf (Italian) parsley	15 mL

1. In a large skillet, heat oil over medium-high heat. Add mushrooms and garlic; cook, stirring often, for 5 minutes or until mushrooms start to brown.

2. Transfer mushroom mixture to one slow cooker stoneware. Sprinkle with Italian seasoning, salt, black pepper and hot pepper flakes to taste.

3. In a small bowl, stir together wine and tomato paste; pour over mushrooms.

4. Cover and cook on Low for 2 to 4 hours or on High for 1 to 2 hours, until hot. Turn to Warm for serving. Sprinkle with oregano just before serving.

Fiery Hot Wings

Makes 8 to 10 servings

Every football party needs a great wing recipe. This will become your go-to, easy-does-it wings-for-a-crowd recipe. Don't sweat the small stuff.

Tip

If desired, add a few drops of hot pepper sauce to the sauce mixture.

Make Ahead

Prepare wings as directed in step 1, cover and refrigerate overnight. The next day, place in stoneware and proceed with the recipe.

• **Rimmed baking sheet, lined with foil**

4 lbs	chicken wings	2 kg
1/3 cup	unsalted butter	75 mL
1	package (1 oz/35 g) taco seasoning mix	1
1 cup	Buffalo wing sauce	250 mL

1. Cut off wing tips and discard. Cut wings at joint into two pieces. Place wings in one slow cooker stoneware.

2. In a small saucepan, melt butter over medium heat. Remove from heat and whisk in taco seasoning and Buffalo sauce. Pour two-thirds of the sauce over wings. Cover and reserve the remaining sauce at room temperature.

3. Cover and cook on Low for 4 to 5 hours or on High for 2 to 2½ hours, until wings are tender and juices run clear when chicken is pierced.

4. Preheat broiler, with rack positioned 4 to 5 inches (10 to 12.5 cm) from heat. Using tongs, carefully lift wings from slow cooker and arrange in a single layer on prepared baking sheet. Discard liquid from stoneware. Brush wings with some of the reserved sauce.

5. Broil for 4 to 5 minutes or until wings are crisp on top. Turn wings and brush with sauce. Broil for 4 to 5 minutes or until crisp.

6. Return wings to stoneware. Turn to Warm for serving.

Citrus-Glazed Wings

Makes 8 to 10 servings

If a recipe features a sweet sauce on meat, rest assured that Kathy will love it. Naturally, this is one of her favorite recipes.

Tips

If desired, substitute drumettes, now available at many grocery stores, for the wings.

These wings are very saucy. Be sure to provide plenty of napkins.

Make Ahead

Prepare wings as directed in step 1, cover and refrigerate overnight. The next day, place in stoneware and proceed with the recipe.

- Rimmed baking sheet, lined with foil

4 lbs	chicken wings	2 kg
6	cloves garlic, minced	6
2 tbsp	minced gingerroot	30 mL
½ cup	orange juice	125 mL
½ cup	liquid honey	125 mL
¼ cup	reduced-sodium soy sauce	60 mL
¼ cup	ketchup	60 mL
2 tbsp	hot pepper sauce	30 mL
	Salt and freshly ground black pepper	

1. Cut off wing tips and discard. Cut wings at joint into two pieces. Place wings in one slow cooker stoneware.

2. In a small bowl, combine garlic, ginger, orange juice, honey, soy sauce, ketchup and hot pepper sauce. Season to taste with salt and black pepper. Pour half the sauce over wings. Cover and reserve the remaining sauce at room temperature.

3. Cover and cook on Low for 4 to 5 hours or on High for 2 to 2½ hours, until wings are tender and juices run clear when chicken is pierced.

4. Preheat broiler with rack positioned 4 to 5 inches (10 to 12.5 cm) from heat. Using tongs, carefully lift wings from slow cooker and arrange in a single layer on prepared baking sheet. Discard liquid from stoneware.

5. Broil for 4 to 5 minutes or until wings are crisp on top. Turn wings and broil for 4 to 5 minutes or until crisp.

6. Return wings to stoneware and drizzle with the reserved sauce. Cover and cook on Low for 30 minutes. Turn to Warm for serving.

Sticky Wings

A little sweet and a little spicy — and absolutely delicious.

Tips

When planning a party, be sure to provide a balance of spicy foods and milder dishes. If the other dishes on your menu are mild, kick up the spice level on these wings by increasing the hot pepper sauce to 1½ to 2 tsp (7 to 10 mL).

These wings are very saucy. Be sure to provide plenty of napkins.

Make Ahead

Prepare wings as directed in step 1, cover and refrigerate overnight. The next day, place in stoneware and proceed with the recipe.

• Rimmed baking sheet, lined with foil

4 lbs	chicken wings	2 kg
1 tsp	garlic powder	5 mL
1 tsp	chili powder	5 mL
1 tsp	salt	5 mL
1½ cups	ketchup	375 mL
½ cup	liquid honey	125 mL
½ cup	red wine vinegar	125 mL
½ cup	light (fancy) molasses	125 mL
1½ tsp	Worcestershire sauce	7 mL
1 tsp	hot pepper sauce	5 mL

1. Cut off wing tips and discard. Cut wings at joint into two pieces. Place wings in one slow cooker stoneware.

2. In a medium bowl, combine garlic powder, chili powder, salt, ketchup, honey, vinegar, molasses, Worcestershire sauce and hot pepper sauce. Pour half the sauce over wings. Cover and reserve the remaining sauce at room temperature.

3. Cover and cook on Low for 4 to 5 hours or on High for 2 to 2½ hours, until wings are tender and juices run clear when chicken is pierced.

4. Preheat broiler with rack positioned 4 to 5 inches (10 to 12.5 cm) from heat. Using tongs, carefully lift wings from slow cooker and arrange in a single layer on prepared baking sheet. Discard liquid from stoneware.

5. Broil for 4 to 5 minutes or until wings are crisp on top. Turn wings and broil for 4 to 5 minutes or until crisp.

6. Return wings to stoneware and drizzle with the reserved sauce. Cover and cook on Low for 30 minutes. Turn to Warm for serving.

Asian Chicken Wings

**Makes 8 to
10 servings**

The sweet-and-sour
flavor of these wings
provides a nice change
from the usual hot-and-
spicy option.

Tip

Sprinkle with 2 finely
chopped green onions
before serving.

Make Ahead

Prepare wings as directed in
step 1, cover and refrigerate
overnight. The next day,
place in stoneware and
proceed with the recipe.

• **Rimmed baking sheet, lined with foil**

4 lbs	chicken wings	2 kg
½ cup	packed brown sugar	125 mL
1 tsp	dry minced (granulated) garlic	5 mL
⅓ cup	reduced-sodium soy sauce	75 mL
¼ cup	ketchup	60 mL
¼ cup	hoisin sauce	60 mL

1. Cut off wing tips and discard. Cut wings at joint into two pieces. Place wings in one slow cooker stoneware.

2. In a small bowl, combine brown sugar, garlic, soy sauce, ketchup and hoisin sauce. Remove ¼ cup (60 mL) of the sauce, cover and reserve at room temperature. Pour the remaining sauce over wings.

3. Cover and cook on Low for 4 to 5 hours or on High for 2 to 2½ hours, until wings are tender and juices run clear when chicken is pierced.

4. Preheat broiler with rack positioned 4 to 5 inches (10 to 12.5 cm) from heat. Using tongs, carefully lift wings from slow cooker and arrange in a single layer on prepared baking sheet. Discard liquid from stoneware. Brush wings with some of the reserved sauce.

5. Broil for 4 to 5 minutes or until wings are crisp on top. Turn wings and brush with sauce. Broil for 4 to 5 minutes or until crisp.

6. Return wings to stoneware. Turn to Warm for serving.

Bacon-Wrapped Chicken Bites

Makes 30 appetizers

In this tasty and surprising appetizer, the chicken bites are flavored with cream cheese and smoky bacon, and the sauce combines orange marmalade and jalapeño peppers. We think it is absolutely fabulous, so we serve it often.

Tip

Garlic- or herb-flavored spreadable cream cheese are other good choices for this recipe.

Make Ahead

Pound chicken until thin, spread with cream cheese and roll in bacon as described in step 3. Cover and refrigerate overnight. Bake rolls and prepare sauce as directed on the day of the party.

- 30 wooden toothpicks
- Rimmed baking sheet, lined with foil

2	jalapeño peppers, seeded and finely chopped	2
2	cloves garlic, minced	2
1/4 tsp	salt	1 mL
1/4 tsp	freshly ground black pepper	1 mL
3/4 cup	orange marmalade	175 mL
1/4 cup	reduced-sodium soy sauce	60 mL
2 lbs	boneless skinless chicken breasts	1 kg
2 tbsp	garden vegetable–flavored spreadable cream cheese	30 mL
10	slices bacon, cut into thirds	10

1. In a deep bowl, soak toothpicks in enough water to cover for about 30 minutes. Meanwhile, preheat oven to 425°F (220°C).

2. In one slow cooker stoneware, combine jalapeños, garlic, salt, pepper, marmalade and soy sauce. Cover and cook on High for 30 minutes.

3. Meanwhile, place chicken between two sheets of plastic wrap and pound until very thin. Spread cream cheese evenly over one side of chicken. Cut chicken into pieces about 2½ by 1½ inches (6 by 4 cm). Starting at a narrow end, roll up each piece like a jelly roll. Wrap each roll in a piece of bacon, securing bacon with a toothpick.

4. Place in a single layer on prepared baking sheet. Bake for 15 to 17 minutes or until chicken is no longer pink inside.

5. Position oven rack about 5 inches (12.5 cm) from heat and preheat broiler. Broil rolls, turning once, for 2 to 3 minutes per side or until bacon is crisp.

6. Spoon most of the sauce from stoneware into a small bowl or measuring cup. Arrange hot chicken rolls in stoneware. Drizzle sauce over top. Cover and cook on High for 30 minutes. Turn to Warm for serving.

Favorite Barbecue Ribs

Makes 8 appetizer servings

In our opinion, Kansas City has the best barbecue on the planet, hands down! We enjoy our barbecue in a variety of ways, but this recipe is one of our favorites.

Tips

If you wish to serve these ribs as an entrée, they'll feed 4 people.

If you want to save two of the slow cooker's stoneware vessels for cooking other dishes for your party, cook the rib sections all together in a 4- to 6-quart slow cooker. After broiling them, place them in one of the Triple Slow Cooker's stoneware vessels and turn to Warm for serving.

If you're not crazy about the characteristic Kansas City smoked flavor, you can omit the liquid smoke.

• **Large rimmed baking sheet, lined with foil**

3 to 4 lbs	baby back pork ribs	1.5 to 2 kg
1/4 to 1/2 tsp	liquid smoke	1 to 2 mL
1 1/4 cups	barbecue sauce, divided	300 mL

1. Cut ribs into three-rib sections. Place about half the rib sections in each of two slow cooker stoneware vessels. Drizzle ribs in both vessels evenly with liquid smoke to taste. Drizzle barbecue sauce evenly over ribs in both vessels, using about 1 cup (250 mL) total.

2. Cover and cook on Low for 7 to 9 hours or on High for 3 1/2 to 4 1/2 hours, until meat is tender.

3. Preheat broiler. Using tongs, carefully remove ribs from slow cooker and arrange, meaty side up, in a single layer on prepared baking sheet. Discard accumulated liquid. Brush ribs with the remaining barbecue sauce.

4. Broil for 5 to 7 minutes or until ribs are crisp (watch carefully to make sure they don't burn). Return ribs to one slow cooker stoneware, cover and turn to Warm for serving.

Asian-Style Ribs

Makes 8 appetizer servings

Not everyone enjoys spicy or barbecue-flavored ribs. Here's a refreshing sweet alternative that's sure to please one and all.

Tips

If you wish to serve these ribs as an entrée, they'll feed 4 people.

If you want to save two of the slow cooker's stoneware vessels for cooking other dishes for your party, cook the rib sections all together in a 4- to 6-quart slow cooker. After broiling them, place them in one of the Triple Slow Cooker's stoneware vessels and turn to Warm for serving.

- **Large rimmed baking sheet, lined with foil**

3 to 4 lbs	baby back pork ribs	1.5 to 2 kg
2 tsp	grated gingerroot	10 mL
½ cup	packed brown sugar	125 mL
1 tbsp	dry minced onion	15 mL
1 tsp	dry minced (granulated) garlic	5 mL
½ tsp	hot pepper flakes	2 mL
½ cup	ketchup	125 mL
¼ cup	liquid honey	60 mL
2 tbsp	reduced-sodium soy sauce	30 mL
2 tbsp	cider vinegar	30 mL
	Salt and freshly ground black pepper	

1. Cut ribs into three-rib pieces. Place about half the rib sections in each of two slow cooker stoneware vessels.

2. In a small bowl, combine ginger, brown sugar, onion, garlic, hot pepper flakes, ketchup, honey, soy sauce and vinegar. Season to taste with salt and black pepper. Measure out ¼ cup (60 mL) sauce, cover and refrigerate. Pour the remaining sauce over the ribs in both vessels, dividing evenly.

3. Cover and cook on Low for 7 to 9 hours or on High for 3½ to 4½ hours, until meat is tender.

4. Preheat broiler. Using tongs, carefully remove ribs from slow cooker and arrange, meaty side up, in a single layer on prepared baking sheet. Discard accumulated liquid. Brush ribs with the reserved sauce.

5. Broil for 5 to 7 minutes or until ribs are crisp (watch carefully to make sure they don't burn). Return ribs to one slow cooker stoneware, cover and turn to Warm for serving.

Zesty Holiday Cocktail Sausages

Makes 12 servings

This recipe is a Wyss family tradition on Christmas Eve, when the entire family gathers to create warm memories.

Tip

If you prefer, you can substitute fully cooked wieners, cut into 1½-inch (4 cm) pieces, for the cocktail sausages.

Make Ahead

Prepare recipe through step 2, cover and refrigerate overnight. Cook as directed.

2	packages (each 13 to 16 oz/ 405 to 500 g) cocktail sausages	2
⅔ cup	packed brown sugar	150 mL
1	jar (12 oz/375 mL) tomato-based chili sauce	1
½ cup	barbecue sauce	125 mL
⅓ cup	bourbon	75 mL
1½ tbsp	Worcestershire sauce	22 mL

1. Place sausages in one slow cooker stoneware.

2. In a small bowl, combine brown sugar, chili sauce, barbecue sauce, bourbon and Worcestershire sauce. Pour over sausages.

3. Cover and cook on Low for 2 to 4 hours or on High for 1 to 2 hours, until hot. Turn to Warm for serving.

Beer-Braised Cocktail Sausages

Makes 12 servings

Give cocktail sausages a new spin with this beer-spiked barbecue sauce.

Tip

You can use any variety of beer in this recipe. A dark stout will provide a strong flavor, while a lager will be lighter.

Make Ahead

Prepare recipe through step 2, cover and refrigerate overnight. Cook as directed.

2	packages (each 13 to 16 oz/ 405 to 500 g) cocktail sausages	2
1/3 cup	packed brown sugar	75 mL
1/2 tsp	garlic powder	2 mL
1 cup	barbecue sauce	250 mL
1/2 cup	beer	125 mL
3 tbsp	Worcestershire sauce	45 mL
1 tbsp	Dijon mustard	15 mL
2 to 3	drops hot pepper sauce	2 to 3

1. Place sausages in one slow cooker stoneware.

2. In a small bowl, combine brown sugar, garlic powder, barbecue sauce, beer, Worcestershire sauce, mustard and hot pepper sauce to taste. Pour over sausages.

3. Cover and cook on Low for 2 to 4 hours or on High for 1 to 2 hours, until hot. Turn to Warm for serving.

Sloppy Joe Sliders

Makes 12 to 14 servings

When the crowd at your party includes a number of children, there is no more perfect dish to serve than this all-time family favorite.

Tip

If you like sweeter sloppy Joes, increase the brown sugar to 1 to 2 tbsp (15 to 30 mL).

Make Ahead

Brown beef and onion, place in a shallow container and refrigerate overnight. In a separate container, combine sauce mixture as directed in step 2; cover and refrigerate. The next day, combine chilled beef mixture and sauce mixture in the stoneware and cook as directed.

2½ lbs	lean ground beef	1.25 kg
1	small onion, finely chopped	1
½	red or green bell pepper, finely chopped	½
1 tbsp	chili powder	15 mL
2 tsp	packed brown sugar	10 mL
1	can (8 oz/227 mL) tomato sauce	1
1 cup	ketchup	250 mL
2 tbsp	Worcestershire sauce	30 mL
2 tbsp	red wine vinegar	30 mL
	Salt and freshly ground black pepper	
12 to 14	slider buns, split and toasted	12 to 14

1. In a large skillet, cook beef, onion and red pepper over medium-high heat, breaking beef up with a spoon and stirring often, for 6 to 8 minutes or until beef is browned and vegetables are tender. Drain off fat.

2. Transfer meat mixture to one slow cooker stoneware. Stir in chili powder, brown sugar, tomato sauce, ketchup, Worcestershire sauce and vinegar. Season to taste with salt and pepper.

3. Cover and cook on Low for 5 to 7 hours or on High for 2½ to 3½ hours, until hot. Turn to Warm for serving.

4. To serve, spoon sloppy Joe mixture onto toasted buns.

Buffalo Sloppy Joe Sliders

Makes 15 to 17 servings

Move over, Buffalo wings. These sloppy Joe sliders are taking over your territory.

Tips

For a milder flavor, replace half of the wing sauce with 1/3 cup (75 mL) ketchup.

Slider buns are now available in many supermarkets and bakeries. If you can't find them, use small bakery rolls or use a cookie cutter to trim hamburger buns a little smaller.

Make Ahead

Brown beef and onion, place in a shallow container and refrigerate overnight. In a separate container, combine sauce mixture as directed in step 2; cover and refrigerate. The next day, combine chilled beef mixture and sauce mixture in the stoneware and cook as directed.

3 lbs	lean ground beef	1.5 kg
1	onion, chopped	1
1 tbsp	dry minced (granulated) garlic	15 mL
1 tbsp	chili powder	15 mL
1	can (8 oz/227 mL) tomato sauce	1
1	can (6 oz/156 mL) tomato paste	1
2/3 cup	Buffalo wing sauce	150 mL
2 tbsp	cider vinegar	30 mL
	Salt and freshly ground black pepper	
15 to 17	slider buns, split and toasted	15 to 17

Sauce

2	stalks celery, finely chopped	2
1	green onion, finely chopped	1
1/2 cup	sour cream	125 mL
1/2 cup	ranch dressing	125 mL
1/3 cup	crumbled blue cheese	75 mL
1 tsp	Buffalo wing sauce	5 mL

1. In a large skillet, cook beef and onion over medium-high heat, breaking beef up with a spoon and stirring often, for 6 to 8 minutes or until beef is browned and onion is tender. Drain off fat.

2. Transfer meat mixture to one slow cooker stoneware. Stir in garlic, chili powder, tomato sauce, tomato paste, wing sauce and vinegar. Season to taste with salt and pepper.

3. Cover and cook on Low for 5 to 7 hours or on High for 2 1/2 to 3 1/2 hours, until hot. Turn to Warm for serving.

4. *Sauce:* Meanwhile, in a small bowl, combine celery, green onion, sour cream, ranch dressing, blue cheese and wing sauce.

5. To serve, spoon sloppy Joe mixture onto bottoms of toasted buns. Spread sauce on top buns, and top sandwiches.

Italian Meatballs

Makes 40 to 42 meatballs

Roxanne belongs to a culinary book club. Once a month, the members prepare recipes from a selected cookbook and discuss food and cooking until the wee hours of the morning. One member, Dee Barwick, shared her recipe for Italian meatballs. This is Roxanne's adaptation for the slow cooker. Thanks, Dee!

Tips

For larger, entrée-sized meatballs, shape the beef mixture into 2-inch (4 cm) balls.

Instead of browning the meatballs in a skillet, you can bake them in a 425°F (220°C) oven. Arrange meatballs on a rimmed baking sheet lined with foil. Bake for 20 to 25 minutes or until no longer pink inside.

	Nonstick baking spray	
2 lbs	lean ground beef	1 kg
4	cloves garlic, minced	4
1 cup	dry bread crumbs with Italian seasoning	250 mL
1/2 cup	freshly grated Parmesan cheese	125 mL
1/4 cup	chopped fresh parsley	60 mL
2 tsp	dried basil	10 mL
4	large eggs, beaten	4
	Salt and freshly ground black pepper	
1/4 cup	olive oil, divided	60 mL
1/2 cup	marinara sauce (store-bought or see recipe, page 111)	125 mL

1. Spray one slow cooker stoneware with baking spray.

2. In a large bowl, combine beef, garlic, bread crumbs, Parmesan, parsley, basil and eggs. Season with salt and pepper. Form into 1½-inch (4 cm) balls.

3. In a large skillet, heat half the oil over medium-high heat. Working in batches, cook meatballs, turning to brown evenly, for 6 to 8 minutes or until no longer pink inside, adding more oil and adjusting heat as necessary between batches. Using tongs, carefully transfer meatballs to prepared stoneware. Pour marinara sauce over meatballs.

Make Ahead

Form and brown meatballs as directed. Spread in a single layer on a tray, cover and refrigerate for up to 1 day. When ready to cook, transfer meatballs to stoneware, cover with plastic wrap and microwave on High for 5 to 7 minutes, stirring halfway through to rearrange meatballs, until steaming hot. Cook as directed in step 4.

4. Cover and cook on Low for 3 to 4 hours or on High for 1 to $1\frac{1}{2}$ hours, until sauce is hot and bubbly. Turn to Warm for serving.

Italian Meatball Sandwich

These meatballs are great on a meatball sandwich. Toast a split hoagie roll, then spoon the cooked meatballs and sauce over the roll. Top with shredded mozzarella cheese and freshly grated Parmesan cheese. Place on a baking sheet and bake in a 375°F (190°C) oven for 8 to 10 minutes or until cheese is melted.

Firehouse Meatballs

Makes 40 to 42 meatballs

The name for these meatballs comes from the sauce's smoky-sweet flavor, which is thanks to the bacon and roasted vegetables.

Tips

For larger, entrée-sized meatballs, shape the beef mixture into 2-inch (4 cm) balls.

Browning the meatballs in the bacon drippings accents the smoky flavor, but feel free to bake them in a 425°F (220°C) oven instead. Arrange meatballs on a rimmed baking sheet lined with foil. Bake for 20 to 25 minutes or until no longer pink inside.

Make sure the meatballs are fully cooked (no longer pink inside) before placing them in the slow cooker stoneware and adding the sauce. Otherwise, they will fall apart easily.

- Food processor or blender

	Nonstick baking spray	
2 lbs	lean ground beef	1 kg
½ cup	dry bread crumbs with Italian seasoning	125 mL
¼ cup	finely chopped onion	60 mL
1 tsp	garlic salt	5 mL
2	large eggs, beaten	2
	Freshly ground black pepper	
4	slices bacon	4
	Vegetable oil (if needed)	
1	can (14 oz/398 mL) fire-roasted diced tomatoes (or regular diced tomatoes), with juice	1
⅓ cup	drained roasted red bell peppers	75 mL
2 tsp	chili powder	10 mL
	Salt	
¼ cup	barbecue sauce	60 mL
1 tsp	Worcestershire sauce	5 mL
1	green onion, finely chopped	1

1. Spray one slow cooker stoneware with baking spray.

2. In a large bowl, combine beef, bread crumbs, onion, garlic salt and eggs. Season with pepper. Form into 1½-inch (4 cm) balls and set aside.

3. In a large skillet, cook bacon over medium heat until crisp. Transfer bacon to a plate lined with paper towels to drain. Reserve drippings in skillet.

Make Ahead

Form and brown meatballs as directed. Spread in a single layer on a tray, cover and refrigerate for up to 1 day. Crumble cooked bacon and refrigerate in a separate airtight container. When ready to cook, transfer meatballs to stoneware, cover with plastic wrap and microwave on High for 5 to 7 minutes, stirring halfway through to rearrange meatballs, until steaming hot. Continue as directed in step 5.

4. Return skillet to medium heat. Working in batches, cook meatballs, turning to brown evenly, for 6 to 8 minutes or until no longer pink inside, adding oil and adjusting heat as necessary between batches. Using tongs, carefully transfer meatballs to prepared stoneware.

5. In food processor, combine tomatoes with juice, roasted peppers, chili powder, salt and pepper to taste, barbecue sauce and Worcestershire sauce; purée until smooth. Pour sauce over meatballs. Crumble bacon and sprinkle on top.

6. Cover and cook on Low for 3 to 4 hours or on High for 1 to 1$\frac{1}{2}$ hours, until meatballs are hot and sauce is bubbly. Turn to Warm for serving. Sprinkle with green onion just before serving.

Tamale Meatballs

Makes 40 to 42 meatballs

Roxanne's dad, Kenny Wyss, adores tamales. She had such fun developing this recipe with her dad in mind, knowing he would savor every bite. Serve over Mexican rice for a hearty dinner.

Tip

For larger, entrée-sized meatballs, shape the beef mixture into 2-inch (4 cm) balls.

Make Ahead

Form and bake meatballs as directed. Spread in a single layer on a tray, cover and refrigerate for up to 1 day. When ready to cook, transfer meatballs to stoneware, cover with plastic wrap and microwave on High for 5 to 7 minutes, stirring halfway through to rearrange meatballs, until steaming hot. Pour in the remaining enchilada sauce and cook as directed in step 5.

- Preheat oven to 425°F (220°C)
- Large rimmed baking sheet, lined with foil

	Nonstick baking spray	
2 lbs	lean ground beef	1 kg
¾ cup	yellow cornmeal	175 mL
1 tbsp	chili powder	15 mL
1 tbsp	ground cumin	15 mL
½ tsp	dry minced (granulated) garlic	2 mL
1	large egg, beaten	1
1	can (28 oz/796 mL) mild enchilada sauce, divided	1

1. Spray one slow cooker stoneware with baking spray.

2. In a large bowl, combine beef, cornmeal, chili powder, cumin, garlic, egg and ⅓ cup (75 mL) of the enchilada sauce. Form into 1½-inch (4 cm) balls. Place at least 1 inch (2.5 cm) apart on prepared baking sheet.

3. Bake in preheated oven for 20 to 25 minutes or until meatballs are no longer pink inside.

4. Using tongs, carefully transfer meatballs to prepared stoneware. Pour in the remaining enchilada sauce.

5. Cover and cook on Low for 3 to 4 hours or on High for 1½ to 2 hours, until meatballs are hot and sauce is bubbly. Turn to Warm for serving.

Variation

Replace half the beef with 1 lb (500 g) sausage (bulk or casings removed).

Tangy Meatballs

Makes 40 to 42 meatballs

These will be an instant hit at your next cocktail party. Make plenty, as no one will be able to resist them.

Tips

For larger, entrée-sized meatballs, shape the beef mixture into 2-inch (4 cm) balls.

Make sure the meatballs are fully cooked (no longer pink inside) before placing them in the slow cooker stoneware and adding the sauce. Otherwise, they will fall apart easily.

Make Ahead

Form and bake meatballs as directed. Spread in a single layer on a tray, cover and refrigerate for up to 1 day. Prepare sauce as directed in step 4, cover and refrigerate separately. When ready to cook, transfer meatballs to stoneware, cover with plastic wrap and microwave on High for 5 to 7 minutes, stirring halfway through to rearrange meatballs, until steaming hot. Top with sauce and cook as directed in step 5.

- **Preheat oven to 425°F (220°C)**
- **Large rimmed baking sheet, lined with foil**

	Nonstick baking spray	
2 lbs	lean ground beef	1 kg
2	green onions, finely chopped	2
4 tsp	grated gingerroot, divided	20 mL
½ cup	panko bread crumbs	125 mL
1	large egg, beaten	1
2 tbsp	reduced-sodium soy sauce, divided	30 mL
1	red bell pepper, finely chopped	1
1 tsp	dry minced (granulated) garlic	5 mL
¼ tsp	hot pepper flakes	1 mL
1	jar (12 oz/340 mL) tomato-based chili sauce	1
1	jar (12 oz/340 mL) apple jelly	1
1 tbsp	rice vinegar	15 mL
3	green onions, thinly sliced	3

1. Spray one slow cooker stoneware with baking spray.

2. In a large bowl, combine beef, chopped green onions, 3 tsp (15 mL) of the ginger, panko, egg and half the soy sauce. Form into 1½-inch (4 cm) balls. Place at least 1 inch (2.5 cm) apart on prepared baking sheet.

3. Bake in preheated oven for 20 to 25 minutes or until meatballs are no longer pink inside. Using tongs, carefully transfer meatballs to prepared stoneware.

4. In a medium bowl, combine red pepper, the remaining ginger, garlic, hot pepper flakes, chili sauce, apple jelly, vinegar and the remaining soy sauce. Pour over meatballs.

5. Cover and cook on Low for 3 to 4 hours or on High for 1½ to 2 hours, until meatballs are hot and sauce is bubbly. Turn to Warm for serving. Sprinkle with sliced green onions just before serving.

Mushroom and Caramelized Onion Bruschetta

Makes 12 servings

We love to serve this recipe. When we featured it at one of our cooking classes, everyone declared it a favorite.

Tips

You may be able to find caramelized onions in jars at well-stocked supermarkets. It's fine to substitute store-bought caramelized onions if you don't have time to make your own.

Gorgonzola is an Italian blue cheese known for its excellent flavor. If it's not available, you can substitute another blue cheese.

To toast the baguette, arrange sliced bread in a single layer on baking sheets. Brush lightly with olive oil. Broil, turning once, until lightly toasted on both sides. Transfer to a basket lined with a cloth to serve.

	Nonstick baking spray	
2 tbsp	olive oil	30 mL
1 lb	button and/or wild mushrooms, thinly sliced	500 g
½ cup	Caramelized Onions (page 158)	125 mL
1 tbsp	minced fresh flat-leaf (Italian) parsley	15 mL
1 tsp	minced fresh thyme	5 mL
	Salt and freshly ground black pepper	
1 cup	shredded fontina cheese	250 mL
½ cup	crumbled Gorgonzola cheese	125 mL
12	toasted baguette or country-style bread slices (see tip, at left)	12

1. Spray one slow cooker stoneware with baking spray.

2. In a large skillet, heat oil over medium-high heat. Add mushrooms and cook, stirring occasionally, for 7 to 10 minutes or until mushrooms are tender and liquid has evaporated.

3. Transfer mushrooms to prepared stoneware. Stir in caramelized onions, parsley and thyme. Season to taste with salt and pepper. Stir in fontina and Gorgonzola.

4. Cover and cook on High for 1 to 2 hours or until cheese is melted. Turn to Warm for serving.

5. To serve, spoon mushroom mixture onto toasted baguette slices.

Artichoke and Goat Cheese Crostini

Makes 20 to 25 servings

The rich flavor of these crostini will remind you of those you might order in an elegant restaurant or trendy bistro.

Tips

For an elegant addition, use a vegetable peeler to cut thin strips from a wedge of Parmesan cheese. Place a bowl of Parmesan slices near the baguette slices so guests can add one or two to their crostini.

When entertaining, use the very best ingredients you can find, especially for cheese. The flavor of goat cheese varies by the brand, so experiment to find the one you prefer. For this recipe, we buy the kind packaged in a tube or disk. Freshly grate Parmesan cheese from a wedge; for the finest flavor, choose Parmigiano-Reggiano.

Make Ahead

You can assemble the artichoke mixture through step 3 early in the day, then cover and refrigerate until you're ready to cook it.

	Nonstick baking spray	
¼ cup	unsalted butter	60 mL
1 lb	button and/or wild mushrooms, thinly sliced	500 g
4	cloves garlic, minced	4
1	can (14 oz/398 mL) artichoke hearts, drained and coarsely chopped	1
1 tsp	dried thyme	5 mL
½ cup	dry white wine	125 mL
	Salt and freshly ground black pepper	
6 oz	soft goat cheese, cut into pieces	175 g
3 oz	cream cheese, cut into ½-inch (1 cm) cubes	90 g
¾ cup	freshly grated Parmesan cheese	175 mL
20 to 25	toasted baguette slices (see tip, page 92)	20 to 25

1. Spray one slow cooker stoneware with nonstick baking spray.

2. In a large skillet, melt butter over medium-high heat. Add mushrooms and garlic; cook, stirring occasionally, for 7 to 10 minutes or until mushrooms are tender and liquid has evaporated.

3. Transfer mushroom mixture to prepared stoneware. Stir in artichokes, thyme and wine. Season to taste with salt and pepper.

4. Cover and cook on High for 1 hour. Stir in goat cheese, cream cheese and Parmesan. Cover and cook on Low for 30 minutes or until cheese is melted. Turn to Warm for serving.

5. To serve, spoon artichoke mixture onto toasted baguette slices.

Caponata Crostini

Makes 25 to 30 servings

This appetizer is fun, slightly different and chock-full of fresh vegetables. It's especially delicious in the summer, when produce is fresh and flavorful.

Tips

The vegetables in this caponata are intended to be warm, but still colorful and tender-crisp.

Leftover caponata is excellent heated and tossed with pasta. It is also wonderful as a panini filling. To make the panini, place 1/3 to 1/2 cup (75 to 125 mL) caponata in a small microwave-safe bowl. Microwave on High for 1 minute or until hot. Lightly butter 2 slices of crusty Italian bread and make a sandwich using the hot caponata as the filling. Add a slice of mozzarella, provolone or another favorite cheese. Grill in a panini press until bread is toasted.

3 tbsp	olive oil	45 mL
1	onion, chopped	1
4	cloves garlic, minced	4
1	red bell pepper, cut into 2- by 1/4-inch (5 by 0.5 cm) strips	1
1	green bell pepper, cut into 2- by 1/4-inch (5 by 0.5 cm) strips	1
1	zucchini (unpeeled), cut lengthwise into quarters, then cut crosswise into 1/2-inch (1 cm) thick slices	1
1	eggplant, peeled and cut into 1-inch (5 cm) cubes	1
1 tbsp	dried Italian seasoning	15 mL
1/4 tsp	hot pepper flakes	1 mL
1	can (14 oz/398 mL) diced tomatoes, with juice	1
1 tbsp	freshly squeezed lemon juice	15 mL
	Salt and freshly ground black pepper	
25 to 30	toasted Italian bread slices or warm pita wedges	25 to 30
	Freshly grated Parmesan cheese	

1. In a large skillet, heat oil over medium-high heat. Add onion and garlic; cook, stirring often, for 3 minutes or until onion is translucent. Add red pepper, green pepper and zucchini; cook, stirring often, for 3 minutes. Add eggplant and cook, stirring often, for about 5 minutes or until vegetables are tender-crisp.

2. Transfer eggplant mixture to one slow cooker stoneware. Stir in Italian seasoning, hot pepper flakes, tomatoes with juice and lemon juice. Season to taste with salt and pepper.

3. Cover and cook on Low for 5 to 6 hours or on High for 2 1/2 to 3 hours, until hot. Turn to Warm for serving.

4. To serve, spoon caponata onto toasted bread slices. Sprinkle with Parmesan.

Oyster Cracker Snacks

Makes about 8 cups (2 L), or 16 servings

These snacks are so tasty and crunchy you might end up making them even when you're not having a party!

Tip

If you have crackers left over, let cool, then store in a sealable food bag at room temperature for up to 2 weeks. Eat them as a snack, or sprinkle them over hot soup.

8 cups	oyster crackers	2 L
1	envelope (1 oz/28 g) powdered ranch salad dressing mix	1
1 tsp	dried dillweed	5 mL
½ tsp	garlic powder	2 mL
¼ tsp	onion powder	1 mL
¼ tsp	lemon pepper or freshly ground black pepper	1 mL
½ cup	vegetable oil	125 mL

1. Place crackers in a large sealable food bag. Add dressing mix, dill, garlic powder, onion powder, lemon pepper and oil. Seal and shake to coat crackers evenly. Pour into one slow cooker stoneware.

2. Cover and cook on Low for 1 hour. Uncover and cook on Low for 1 hour, stirring occasionally. Turn to Warm for serving.

Scrumptious Sweet and Spicy Nuts

Makes about 5 cups (1.25 L)

Sweet and spicy, crunchy and utterly addictive — what's not to love about this snack?

Tip

If you have nuts left over, let cool, then store in a sealable food bag at room temperature for up to 1 month. Pack them in small bags for lunch boxes or to take as a snack when traveling. They also make a great addition to a salad.

1 tbsp	unsalted butter	15 mL
3 cups	pecan halves	750 mL
2 cups	blanched whole almonds	500 mL
2 tbsp	pure maple syrup	30 mL
1 tsp	coarse kosher salt	5 mL
½ tsp	cayenne pepper	2 mL

1. Rub the inside of one slow cooker stoneware with butter. Add pecans and almonds to stoneware. Drizzle with maple syrup and stir to coat evenly. Sprinkle with salt and cayenne.

2. Cover and cook on High for 30 minutes. Uncover and cook on High for 1½ to 2 hours, stirring every 30 minutes, until nuts are hot, glazed and beginning to dry. Turn to Warm for serving.

Graduation Gathering

For full menu and party plans, see page 39

Vidalia Onion Dip (page 57)
Tamale Meatballs (page 90)
Favorite Barbecue Ribs (page 80)

New Year's Eve

For full menu and party plans, see page 22

Cheesy Black-Eyed Pea Dip (page 58)

Gruyère and Wild Rice Dip (page 63)

Artichoke and Goat Cheese Crostini
(page 93)

Valentine's Day

For full menu and party plans, see page 25

Hearts of Palm Dip (page 62)
Beef Burgundy (page 120)
Winter Salad (page 161)
Elegant Chocolate Fondue (page 164)

Overnight Guests

For full menu and party plans, see page 34

Overnight Fruited Oatmeal (page 140)

Old-Fashioned Warm Fruit Compote
(page 159)

Biscuits and Gravy (page 138)

Cinco de Mayo

For full menu and party plans, see page 36

Tex-Mex Spinach Dip (page 59)

Chipotle Beef with Fresh Tomato Salsa
(page 116)

Chicken con Queso (page 133)

Derby Day

For full menu and party plans, see page 37

Strawberry Spinach Salad (page 160)

Hot Browns (page 134)

Parmesan Herb Potato Casserole
(page 144)

Hot Fudge Sauce (page 171)

Mother's Day

For full menu and party plans, see page 38

Hot Corn Dip (page 57)

New Orleans Spicy Barbecue Shrimp
(page 136)

Strawberry Rhubarb Dessert (page 176)

Baby Shower

For full menu and party plans, see page 40

Oyster Cracker Snacks (page 95)
Bacon-Wrapped Chicken Bites (page 79)
Creamy Caramel Fondue (page 167)

Father's Day

For full menu and party plans, see page 41

Bacon Cheese Fondue (page 71)
Beer-Braised Brats (page 130)
Tangy Red Cabbage (page 157)

Games Night

For full menu and party plans, see page 46

Citrus-Glazed Wings (page 76)
Firehouse Meatballs (page 88)
Cuban Pork Sandwiches with Cilantro
Mayonnaise (page 128)

Halloween

For full menu and party plans, see page 47

Thanksgiving

For full menu and party plans, see page 49

Winter Salad (page 161)
Savory Sage Bread Dressing (page 142)
Mashed Potatoes (page 143)
Roasted Sweet Potatoes (page 146)

Tailgate Party

For full menu and party plans, see page 44

Buffalo Chicken Dip (page 66)
Sticky Wings (page 77)
Hot-and-Spicy Chili (page 105)

Soups, Chilis and Sauces

French Onion Soup

**Makes 6 to
8 servings**

Caramelizing the onions in a slow cooker makes this dish so easy to prepare you'll want to serve it often.

Tips

Varieties of sweet onions include Vidalia, Walla Walla and Maui. Some are quite large. For this recipe, fill the slow cooker with thinly sliced onions to just below the lid seat. Typically, this will be about 4 or 5 sweet onions but will depend on the variety and size of onion you use. Be sure that the lid rests securely on the slow cooker (do not overfill). The onions will cook down as they caramelize so you will have room for the broth.

Slow cooker stoneware should not be exposed to rapid, extreme temperature changes. For this recipe, be sure the broth is at room temperature before adding it to the stoneware. Do not add cold liquid to hot stoneware, and never place the stoneware under a broiler.

• **Baking sheet, lined with foil**

4 to 5	sweet yellow onions, thinly sliced (see tip, at left)	4 to 5
¼ tsp	dried thyme	1 mL
3 tbsp	olive oil	45 mL
2 tbsp	unsalted butter	30 mL
5¼ cups	reduced-sodium ready-to-use beef broth, at room temperature (see tip, at left)	1.3 L
2 tbsp	dry sherry	30 mL
	Salt and freshly ground black pepper	
6 to 8	slices French bread (about ¾ inch/ 2 cm thick)	6 to 8
6 to 8	slices Gruyère or Swiss cheese	6 to 8
	Freshly grated Parmesan cheese	

1. In one slow cooker stoneware, combine onions, thyme, oil and butter. Cover and cook on High for 6 to 8 hours or until onions are golden brown.

2. Stir in broth and sherry. Season to taste with salt and pepper. Cover and cook on High for 30 minutes. Turn to Warm for serving.

3. Just before serving, preheat broiler. Arrange bread slices on prepared baking sheet. Toast under broiler, turning once, until golden brown on both sides. Cut Gruyère slices to fit on bread. Place a slice on each piece of toast and sprinkle with Parmesan. Broil just until cheese is melted.

4. To serve, ladle soup into bowls and top each with a slice of cheese-covered toast.

Roasted Tomato Basil Soup

Makes 6 to 8 servings

During the heat of summer, when tomatoes are prolific and you don't want to heat up the kitchen, try this light, refreshing soup. It will rival any you have had at a restaurant.

Tip

If you don't own an immersion blender, carefully ladle the tomato mixture into an upright blender or food processor (you may need to do more than one batch) and purée until smooth. Make sure to let the mixture cool slightly first, or vent the cover to avoid steam buildup.

● **Immersion blender**

2¼ to 2½ lbs	tomatoes (about 5 medium to large)	1.125 to 1.25 kg
5	cloves garlic, halved	5
1	onion, cut into thin wedges	1
2 tbsp	olive oil	30 mL
1 tbsp	dried basil	15 mL
1 tsp	salt	5 mL
½ tsp	coarsely ground black pepper	2 mL
¼ tsp	hot pepper flakes	1 mL
3 tbsp	minced fresh basil, divided	45 mL
1	can (28 oz/796 mL) crushed tomatoes	1
1 cup	ready-to-use vegetable broth	250 mL

1. Cut tomatoes into wedges and remove cores and most of the seeds. Place in one slow cooker stoneware. Stir in garlic, onion, oil, dried basil, salt, black pepper and hot pepper flakes.

2. Cover and cook on High for 4½ to 5½ hours, until tomatoes and onion are tender. Turn slow cooker off and let cool slightly.

3. Add 2 tbsp (30 mL) of the fresh basil to the stoneware and, using the immersion blender, blend until smooth. Stir in crushed tomatoes and broth.

4. Cover and cook on Low for 1 to 2 hours or until hot. Turn to Warm for serving.

5. To serve, ladle soup into bowls and sprinkle with the remaining fresh basil.

Variation

Cream of Tomato Basil Soup: Omit the vegetable broth. Stir in ½ to 1 cup (125 mL to 250 mL) half-and-half (10%) cream during the last 20 minutes of cooking in step 4.

Beer and Cheese Soup

**Makes 6 to
8 servings**

Build a fire in the
fireplace and invite
your guests to sip this
flavorful soup while
warming up.

Tips

You can use any type of
beer in this recipe. A lager is
known for a crisp, dry flavor,
while a dark stout or ale will
give the soup a more robust
flavor.

This recipe can also be
served as a fondue. Thin it,
if desired, with a little more
beer or milk. Accompany
with crusty bread cubes,
pretzels or smoked cocktail
sausages for dipping.

1	small onion, chopped	1
1	carrot, chopped	1
1	stalk celery, chopped	1
1	small red bell pepper, chopped	1
¼ tsp	salt (or to taste)	1 mL
½ tsp	freshly ground black pepper	2 mL
3⅔ cups	reduced-sodium ready-to-use chicken broth	900 mL
2 tbsp	unsalted butter	30 mL
⅓ cup	all-purpose flour	75 mL
⅓ cup	cold water	75 mL
8 oz	cream cheese, softened and cut into ½-inch (1 cm) cubes	250 g
2 cups	shredded Cheddar cheese	500 mL
1 cup	beer	250 mL
	Crumbled crisply cooked bacon	
	Sliced green onions	

1. In one slow cooker stoneware, combine onion, carrot, celery, red pepper, salt, pepper, broth and butter.

2. Cover and cook on Low for 7 to 9 hours or on High for 3½ to 4½ hours, until vegetables are tender.

3. In a small bowl, stir together flour and cold water to make a smooth paste. Stir into soup, along with cream cheese, Cheddar and beer. Cover and cook on High for 30 to 60 minutes, stirring once halfway through, until cheese is melted and soup is hot. Turn to Warm for serving.

4. To serve, ladle soup into cups or bowls and sprinkle with bacon and green onions.

Chicken Tortilla Soup

Makes 6 to 8 servings

We both enjoy Chicken Tortilla Soup, but of the two of us, Roxanne is a special fan. She not only serves it to her family, but will often make a batch to take to a friend or neighbor in need of a nourishing meal or a little cheering up.

Tips

Another good topping for this soup is chopped avocado. To keep it from discoloring after you chop it, toss it in freshly squeezed lime juice.

For added color and flavor, add ½ cup (125 mL) frozen corn kernels with the red pepper.

2 tbsp	vegetable oil	30 mL
12 oz	boneless skinless chicken breasts, cut into ½-inch (1 cm) pieces	375 g
2	6-inch (15 cm) corn tortillas, torn into bite-size pieces	2
1	jalapeño pepper, seeded and chopped	1
½	onion, chopped	½
½	red bell pepper, chopped	½
4 tsp	ground cumin	20 mL
1 tbsp	dry minced (granulated) garlic	15 mL
1 tbsp	chili powder	15 mL
⅛ tsp	cayenne pepper (or to taste)	0.5 mL
1	can (14 oz/398 mL) diced tomatoes, with juice	1
1	can (8 oz/227 mL) tomato sauce	1
3½ cups	reduced-sodium ready-to-use chicken broth	875 mL
	Salt and freshly ground black pepper	
	Minced fresh cilantro, shredded Cheddar cheese, sour cream and/or crushed tortilla chips	

1. In a large skillet, heat oil over medium-high heat. Add chicken and cook, stirring often, for 5 to 7 minutes or until lightly browned on all sides.

2. Transfer chicken to one slow cooker stoneware. Stir in tortillas, jalapeño, onion, red pepper, cumin, garlic, chili powder, cayenne, tomatoes with juice, tomato sauce and broth. Season to taste with salt and black pepper.

3. Cover and cook on Low for 6 to 8 hours or on High for 3 to 4 hours, until chicken is no longer pink inside and vegetables are tender. Turn to Warm for serving.

4. To serve, ladle soup into bowls and top with cilantro, Cheddar, sour cream and tortilla chips as desired.

Asian Chicken Soup

This light and flavorful soup will remind you of soup served in Asian restaurants — especially when topped with fried wontons.

Tip

To deep-fry wonton wrappers, preheat a deep fryer filled with vegetable oil to 350°F (180°C) according to the manufacturer's directions. Cut each wonton wrapper into three strips. Fry wonton strips, in batches as necessary, for 30 to 60 seconds or just until golden. Remove with a slotted spoon and drain on a plate lined with paper towels. If preparing ahead, let cool completely, then store between layers of paper towels in an airtight container at room temperature for up to 1 day. When ready to serve, arrange on a baking sheet and bake at 375°F (190°C) for 10 to 15 minutes or until warm and crisp.

1 lb	boneless skinless chicken breasts, cut into 1/2-inch (1 cm) cubes	500 g
12	large mushrooms, thickly sliced	12
1/2 cup	diagonally sliced celery	125 mL
3 2/3 cups	reduced-sodium ready-to-use chicken broth	900 mL
1 tbsp	reduced-sodium soy sauce	15 mL
	Freshly ground black pepper	
2 tbsp	cornstarch	30 mL
2 tbsp	freshly squeezed lemon juice	30 mL
	Sliced green onions	
	Fried wontons (see tip, at left)	

1. In one slow cooker stoneware, combine chicken, mushrooms, celery, broth and soy sauce. Season to taste with pepper.

2. Cover and cook on Low for 6 to 8 hours or on High for 3 to 4 hours, until chicken is no longer pink inside and vegetables are tender.

3. In a small bowl, stir together cornstarch and lemon juice. Stir into soup. Cover and cook on High for 30 minutes. Turn to Warm for serving.

4. To serve, ladle into bowls and sprinkle with green onions and fried wontons.

Variation

Substitute 1 lb (500 g) boneless skinless turkey breast, cut into 1/2-inch (1 cm) cubes, for the chicken.

Tuscan Beef and Bean Soup

Makes 6 to 8 servings

The flavors of the Tuscan countryside, including an array of vegetables, beans, garlic and herbs, are captured in this wonderful soup.

Tip

If you prefer, you can substitute ½ cup (125 mL) frozen cut green beans, partially thawed, for the zucchini.

Make Ahead

Brown beef, place in a shallow container and refrigerate until cold. Once it's chilled, proceed with step 2; cover and refrigerate overnight. Cook as directed.

8 oz	lean ground beef	250 g
1	carrot, chopped	1
1	stalk celery, chopped	1
½	onion, chopped	½
1 tsp	dried Italian seasoning	5 mL
1 tsp	dry minced (granulated) garlic	5 mL
⅛ tsp	hot pepper flakes	0.5 mL
1	can (14 oz/398 mL) diced tomatoes, with juice	1
1¾ cups	reduced-sodium ready-to-use beef broth	425 mL
½ cup	water	125 mL
	Salt and freshly ground black pepper	
1	can (14 to 19 oz/398 to 540 mL) dark red kidney beans, drained and rinsed	1
½ cup	chopped zucchini (unpeeled)	125 mL
2 tbsp	minced fresh flat-leaf (Italian) parsley	30 mL
	Freshly grated Parmesan cheese	

1. In a large skillet, cook beef over medium-high heat, breaking it up with a spoon and stirring often, for 6 to 8 minutes or until no longer pink. Drain off fat.

2. Transfer beef to one slow cooker stoneware. Stir in carrot, celery, onion, Italian seasoning, garlic, hot pepper flakes, tomatoes with juice, broth and water. Season to taste with salt and black pepper.

3. Cover and cook on Low for 6 to 8 hours or on High for 3 to 4 hours, until beef and vegetables are tender. Stir in beans, zucchini and parsley. Cover and cook on High for 1 hour or until zucchini is tender. Turn to Warm for serving.

4. To serve, ladle into bowls and sprinkle with Parmesan.

All-Time Favorite Chili

Makes 6 to 8 servings

For many years, we worked with a Midwestern chili seasoning company. Traveling around the United States, we quickly realized we could tell where someone is from by the kind of chili they prefer. We were raised in the Midwest, so our favorite chili is milder than some and always includes kidney beans.

Tips

Accompany this chili with bowls of shredded Cheddar cheese, chopped onions, sliced jalapeño peppers and/or other favorite chili toppings.

Some folks say it isn't chili if it has beans in it. Omit the beans if you prefer.

Make Ahead

Brown beef and onion, place in a shallow container and refrigerate until cold. Once it's chilled, proceed with step 2; cover and refrigerate overnight. Cook as directed.

2 lbs	lean ground beef	1 kg
1	onion, chopped	1
1	can (14 oz/398 mL) diced tomatoes, with juice	1
1	can (10 oz/284 mL) diced tomatoes and green chiles, with juice	1
3 tbsp	chili powder	45 mL
1 tbsp	dry minced (granulated) garlic	15 mL
2 tsp	ground cumin	10 mL
	Salt and freshly ground black pepper	
1	can (14 to 19 oz/398 to 540 mL) red, kidney, pinto or black beans, drained and rinsed	1

1. In a large skillet, cook beef and onion over medium-high heat, breaking beef up with a spoon and stirring often, for 6 to 8 minutes or until beef is no longer pink and onion is tender. Drain off fat.

2. Transfer beef mixture to one slow cooker stoneware. Stir in tomatoes with juice, tomatoes and chiles with juice, chili powder, garlic and cumin. Season to taste with salt and pepper. Stir in beans.

3. Cover and cook on Low for 6 to 8 hours or on High for 3 to 4 hours, until hot and bubbly. Turn to Warm for serving.

Hot-and-Spicy Chili

Makes 6 to 8 servings

You and your guests will be pleasantly surprised by the crunchy topping on this chili. It is fun and adds great flavor, so don't be tempted to eliminate it.

Tip

Chili beans are seasoned with chile peppers and other seasonings. The flavor and type of bean you choose may vary with your preferences and what is available in your region. Most chili beans are packed in a flavorful sauce, which is added to the chili with the beans. If you're not sure how spicy a brand is, choose a mild or medium flavor, then add a few drops of hot pepper sauce to the chili just before serving if you want more heat. If chili beans are not available in your area, substitute other canned beans, such as red, kidney or pinto beans, drained and rinsed.

Make Ahead

Brown beef and onion, place in a shallow container and refrigerate until cold. Once it's chilled, proceed with step 3; cover and refrigerate overnight. Cook as directed.

4	slices bacon	4
2½ lbs	lean ground beef	1.25 kg
1	onion, chopped	1
3 tbsp	chili powder	45 mL
1 tbsp	ground cumin	15 mL
1 tbsp	packed brown sugar	15 mL
1	can (15 oz/425 mL) medium-heat chili beans (see tip, at left)	1
1	can (6 oz/156 mL) tomato paste	1
1½ cups	medium salsa	375 mL
¼ cup	chopped drained pickled jalapeño peppers	60 mL
	Salt and freshly ground black pepper	
¾ cup	canned french-fried onion rings	175 mL
1 cup	shredded Cheddar cheese	250 mL

1. In a large skillet, cook bacon over medium heat until crisp. Transfer bacon to a plate lined with paper towels to drain.

2. Add beef and onion to the fat remaining in the pan, increase heat to medium-high and cook, breaking beef up with a spoon and stirring often, for 6 to 8 minutes or until beef is no longer pink and onion is tender. Drain off fat.

3. Transfer beef mixture to one slow cooker stoneware. Stir in chili powder, cumin, brown sugar, beans, tomato paste, salsa and jalapeños. Season to taste with salt and pepper. Crumble bacon and stir into chili.

4. Cover and cook on Low for 6 to 8 hours or on High for 3 to 4 hours, until hot and bubbly. Turn to Warm for serving. Sprinkle with onion rings and cheese just before serving.

Champion Chili

Makes 8 servings

This chili is worthy of a blue ribbon and makes a great addition to any game day activity.

Tips

Chili seasoning is a blend of chili powder and other seasonings, such as garlic powder, ground cumin, dried oregano, salt and ground black pepper. If you can't find it, replace it in this recipe with 3 to 4 tbsp (45 to 60 mL) chili powder, 1 tsp (5 mL) ground cumin, 1/2 tsp (2 mL) dried oregano and salt and pepper to taste.

If you prefer, you can substitute a 14- to 19-oz (398 to 540 mL) can of kidney beans, drained and rinsed, for the chili beans.

Make Ahead

Brown beef, sausage and onion, place in a shallow container and refrigerate until cold. Once it's chilled, proceed with step 2; cover and refrigerate overnight. Cook as directed.

1 lb	lean ground beef	500 g
1 lb	pork sausage (bulk or casings removed)	500 g
1	onion, chopped	1
1	package (1 oz/30 g) chili seasoning (see tip, at left)	1
1½ tsp	dry minced (granulated) garlic	7 mL
1	can (15 oz/425 mL) medium-heat chili beans (see tip, page 105)	1
1	can (14 oz/398 mL) diced tomatoes, with juice	1
1 cup	picante sauce or salsa	250 mL
	Shredded Cheddar cheese (optional)	

1. In a large skillet, cook beef, sausage and onion over medium-high heat, breaking meat up with a spoon and stirring often, for 6 to 8 minutes or until meat is no longer pink. Drain off fat.

2. Transfer meat mixture to one slow cooker stoneware. Stir in chili seasoning, garlic, beans, tomatoes with juice and picante sauce.

3. Cover and cook on Low for 6 to 8 hours or on High for 3 to 4 hours, until hot and bubbly. Turn to Warm for serving.

4. To serve, ladle into bowls and sprinkle with Cheddar cheese.

Steak Fajita Chili

Makes 8 servings

Two great favorites —
chili and fajitas — in one
dish! Serve in bowls
or spoon into warm
tortillas. Either way, it's
a winner.

Tips

Browning the meat in
batches helps you avoid
crowding the skillet,
which would cause the
beef to steam instead of
browning nicely.

It is easier to thinly slice icy
cold meat. Place the steak
in the freezer for about
30 minutes, just until it's
icy cold, then thinly slice it
across the grain.

Accompany this chili with
bowls of sour cream,
guacamole, shredded
cheese and/or salsa. Other
toppings might include
sliced jalapeño peppers,
sliced green onions or pico
de gallo.

Make Ahead

Brown steak, place in a
shallow container and
refrigerate until cold. Once
it's chilled, proceed with
step 2; cover and refrigerate
overnight. Cook as directed.

2 tbsp	vegetable oil (approx.), divided	30 mL
2 lbs	beef flank or skirt steak, cut into thin strips	1 kg
1	onion, finely chopped	1
1	red or green bell pepper, cut into strips	1
3 tbsp	chili powder	45 mL
1 tbsp	ground cumin	15 mL
1 tbsp	dry minced (granulated) garlic	15 mL
1	can (14 to 19 oz/398 to 540 mL) black beans, drained and rinsed	1
1	can (10 oz/284 mL) diced tomatoes and green chiles, with juice	1
¼ cup	picante sauce or salsa	60 mL
	Salt and freshly ground black pepper	
	Crushed tortilla chips or warm flour tortillas	

1. In a large skillet, heat half the oil over medium-high heat. Cook steak in 2 or 3 batches, stirring often, for 6 to 8 minutes or until browned, adding more oil between batches as necessary.

2. Transfer steak to one slow cooker stoneware. Stir in onion, red pepper, chili powder, cumin, garlic, beans, tomatoes and chiles with juice, and picante sauce. Season to taste with salt and pepper.

3. Cover and cook on Low for 6 to 8 hours or on High for 3 to 4 hours, until beef and vegetables are tender and chili is hot and bubbly. Turn to Warm for serving.

4. To serve, ladle into bowls and top with tortilla chips, or spoon into tortillas and roll up.

White Chicken Chili

Makes 6 servings

A fun party idea is to serve three different chilis in the Triple Slow Cooker. Be sure to include this one, then select two others, such as the All-Time Favorite Chili (page 104) and the Hot-and-Spicy Chili (page 105). Your guests can select the type of chili they prefer. Remember to set out all kinds of chili toppings!

Tips

If you cannot find canned white shoepeg corn kernels, substitute regular corn kernels.

Another topping we enjoy with this chili is crushed tortilla chips.

2 tbsp	olive oil	30 mL
1 lb	boneless skinless chicken breasts, cut into $\frac{1}{2}$ inch (1 cm) cubes	500 g
3	cloves garlic, minced	3
1	onion, chopped	1
1	can (15 to 16 oz/425 to 500 mL) white shoepeg corn kernels	1
1	can (4 oz/127 mL) chopped mild green chiles	1
2 tsp	ground cumin	10 mL
2 tsp	dried oregano	10 mL
$\frac{1}{2}$ tsp	salt	2 mL
$\frac{1}{4}$ tsp	freshly ground black pepper	1 mL
$\frac{1}{8}$ tsp	cayenne pepper	0.5 mL
$3\frac{2}{3}$ cups	reduced-sodium ready-to-use chicken broth	900 mL
$\frac{1}{4}$ cup	salsa verde	60 mL
1	can (14 to 19 oz/398 to 540 mL) Great Northern or cannellini beans, drained and rinsed	1
2 tbsp	minced fresh cilantro	30 mL
	Shredded Monterey Jack cheese	
2	green onions, chopped	2

1. In a large skillet, heat oil over medium-high heat. Add chicken, garlic and onion; cook, stirring often, for about 5 minutes or until chicken is browned on all sides and onion is tender.

2. Transfer chicken mixture to one slow cooker stoneware. Stir in corn, green chiles, cumin, oregano, salt, black pepper, cayenne, broth and salsa verde.

Make Ahead

Cook chicken and vegetables as directed in step 1, place in a shallow container and refrigerate until cold. Once they're chilled, proceed with step 2; cover and refrigerate overnight. Cook as directed.

3. Cover and cook on Low for 5 to 7 hours or on High for $2\frac{1}{2}$ to $3\frac{1}{2}$ hours, until chicken is tender and chili is hot and bubbly. Stir in beans and cook on High for 30 minutes. Turn to Warm for serving. Stir in cilantro just before serving.

4. To serve, ladle into bowls and sprinkle with cheese and green onions.

Red, White and Blue Chili

Makes 6 to 8 servings

Red and white beans and a topping of crunchy blue corn chips make this chili unique and delicious.

Tip

Blue corn exists naturally, and more blue corn products are now on the market. Give blue corn chips a try. If you can't find them, substitute yellow or white tortilla chips or corn chips.

Make Ahead

Cook vegetables as directed in step 1, place in a shallow container and refrigerate until cold. Once they're chilled, proceed with step 2; cover and refrigerate overnight. Cook as directed.

2 tbsp	vegetable oil	30 mL
1	stalk celery, chopped	1
$\frac{1}{2}$	onion, chopped	$\frac{1}{2}$
$\frac{1}{2}$	green bell pepper, chopped	$\frac{1}{2}$
8 oz	smoked sausage, cut into $\frac{1}{2}$-inch (1 cm) thick slices	250 g
8 oz	cooked ham, cut into $\frac{1}{2}$-inch (1 cm) cubes	250 g
2 tbsp	chili powder	30 mL
1 tbsp	dry minced (granulated) garlic	15 mL
2 tsp	ground cumin	10 mL
$\frac{1}{8}$ tsp	cayenne pepper	0.5 mL
	Salt and freshly ground black pepper	
1	can (14 to 19 oz/398 to 540 mL) red kidney beans, drained and rinsed	1
1	can (14 to 19 oz/398 to 540 mL) Great Northern beans, drained and rinsed	1
$3\frac{2}{3}$ cups	reduced-sodium ready-to-use chicken broth	900 mL
	Blue corn chips	

1. In a large skillet, heat oil over medium-high heat. Add celery, onion and green pepper; cook, stirring often, for 5 minutes or until tender.

2. Transfer onion mixture to one slow cooker stoneware. Stir in sausage, ham, chili powder, garlic, cumin and cayenne. Season to taste with salt and black pepper. Stir in kidney beans, Great Northern beans and broth.

3. Cover and cook on Low for 5 to 7 hours or on High for $2\frac{1}{2}$ to $3\frac{1}{2}$ hours, until hot and bubbly. Turn to Warm for serving.

4. To serve, ladle into bowls and top with blue corn tortilla chips.

Marinara Sauce

**Makes about
9 cups (2.25 L)**

This red sauce has so
many possibilities. Use
it to top your favorite
hot cooked pasta, then
freeze leftovers for
countless uses, such as
pizza topping, calzone
filling or a flavorful
addition to soup.

Tips

If you prefer, you can omit
the wine.

We like to keep marinara
sauce in the freezer, ready
to use in other recipes. Ladle
into airtight containers,
leaving 1 inch (2.5 cm)
headspace for expansion,
label and freeze for up to
6 months. Thaw in the
refrigerator or microwave
before use.

Make Ahead

Prepare sauce through
step 2, cover and refrigerate
overnight. Cook as directed.

1 tbsp	olive oil	15 mL
1 cup	diced onion	250 mL
8	cloves garlic, minced	8
2	bay leaves	2
1/4 cup	minced fresh parsley	60 mL
1 tbsp	granulated sugar	15 mL
2 tsp	dried basil	10 mL
1 1/2 tsp	dried oregano	7 mL
1/2 tsp	salt	2 mL
1/2 tsp	coarsely ground black pepper	2 mL
1	can (28 oz/796 mL) crushed tomatoes	1
1	can (28 oz/796 mL) tomato purée	1
1	can (6 oz/156 mL) tomato paste	1
1/2 cup	dry red wine	125 mL
1/4 cup	water	60 mL

1. In a medium skillet, heat oil over medium-high heat.
   Add onion and garlic; cook, stirring often, for about
   5 minutes or until onion is tender.

2. Transfer onion mixture to one slow cooker stoneware.
   Stir in bay leaves, parsley, sugar, basil, oregano, salt,
   pepper, crushed tomatoes, tomato purée, tomato paste,
   wine and water (stir gently, as the stoneware will be
   very full).

3. Cover and cook on Low for 5 to 7 hours or on High for
   2 1/2 to 3 1/2 hours, until hot and bubbly. Discard bay
   leaves. Turn to Warm for serving.

Bolognese Sauce

**Makes about
5 cups (1.25 L)**

Traditional and
always so very good,
Bolognese sauce is a
favorite. Serve over hot
cooked pasta.

Make Ahead

Brown beef, onion and
garlic, place in a shallow
container and refrigerate
until cold. Once it's chilled,
proceed with step 2; cover
and refrigerate overnight.
Cook as directed.

1 lb	lean ground beef	500 g
½ cup	finely chopped yellow onion	125 mL
4	cloves garlic, minced	4
1	bay leaf	1
2 tbsp	minced fresh parsley	30 mL
1 tsp	granulated sugar	5 mL
1 tsp	dried oregano	5 mL
1 tsp	dried basil	5 mL
1	can (14.5 oz/398 mL) crushed tomatoes (or 1⅔ cups/400 mL)	1
1	can (10.75 oz/300 mL) tomato purée (or 1¼ cups/300 mL)	1
1	can (6 oz/156 mL) tomato paste	1
⅓ cup	dry red wine	175 mL
3 tbsp	water	45 mL
	Salt and freshly ground black pepper	

1. In a medium skillet, cook beef, onion and garlic over medium-high heat, breaking beef up with a spoon and stirring often, for 6 to 8 minutes or until beef is no longer pink and onion is tender. Drain off fat.

2. Transfer beef mixture to one slow cooker stoneware. Stir in bay leaf, parsley, sugar, oregano, basil, crushed tomatoes, tomato purée, tomato paste, wine and water. Season to taste with salt and pepper.

3. Cover and cook on Low for 5 to 7 hours or on High for 2½ to 3½ hours, until hot and bubbly. Discard bay leaf. Turn to Warm for serving.

Variation

Substitute Italian sausage (bulk or removed from casings) for the ground beef.

Eggplant Pasta Sauce

Makes about 6¹⁄₂ cups (1.625 L)

We both love eggplant and especially like it in this rich and tasty pasta sauce. Serve over hot cooked pasta and sprinkle each serving with freshly grated Parmesan cheese.

Tip

The eggplants most commonly available are smooth-skinned and deep purple. The flesh discolors rapidly once cut, so peel and cut the eggplants just before cooking.

¹⁄₄ cup	olive oil, divided	60 mL
2	eggplants (about 2 lbs/1 kg total), peeled and cut into 1-inch (2.5 cm) cubes	2
1	onion, chopped	1
2 tsp	dry minced (granulated) garlic	10 mL
1¹⁄₂ tsp	dried basil	7 mL
1 tsp	dried oregano	5 mL
¹⁄₂ tsp	salt	2 mL
¹⁄₄ tsp	freshly ground black pepper	1 mL
1	can (28 oz/796 mL) crushed tomatoes	1
¹⁄₄ cup	dry red wine	60 mL
2 tbsp	minced fresh basil	30 mL

1. In a large skillet, heat half the oil over medium-high heat. Add half each of the eggplant and onion; cook, stirring often, for 4 minutes or until eggplant is starting to brown. Transfer to one slow cooker stoneware. Repeat with remaining oil, eggplant and onion.

2. Stir in garlic, dried basil, oregano, salt, pepper, tomatoes and wine.

3. Cover and cook on Low for 6 to 7 hours or on High for 3 to 3¹⁄₂ hours, until vegetables are tender and sauce is hot and bubbly. Turn to Warm for serving. Stir in fresh basil just before serving.

Chicken and Mushroom Alfredo Sauce

Makes 6 to 8 servings

This creamy Alfredo sauce, packed with chicken and Parmesan cheese, rivals anything served in the best Italian restaurants, yet it is so easy to prepare. Making it in the slow cooker means there's no last-minute rush, so it's perfect for entertaining. Serve over hot cooked pasta.

Tip

Sprinkle with additional Parmesan cheese just before serving.

2 tbsp	unsalted butter	30 mL
8 oz	sliced mushrooms	250 g
1½ lbs	boneless skinless chicken breasts, cut into 2- by 1-inch (5 by 2.5 cm) strips	750 g
2	cloves garlic, minced	2
	Salt and freshly ground black pepper	
2	jars (each 16 oz/500 mL) Alfredo sauce	2
½ cup	freshly grated Parmesan cheese	125 mL

1. In a large skillet, melt butter over medium-high heat. Add mushrooms and cook, stirring, for about 5 minutes or until tender.

2. Transfer mushrooms to one slow cooker stoneware. Stir in chicken and garlic. Season with salt and pepper. Stir in Alfredo sauce.

3. Cover and cook on Low for 5 to 6 hours or on High for 2½ to 3 hours, until chicken is no longer pink inside and sauce is hot and bubbly. Stir in Parmesan. Turn to Warm for serving.

Variation

Add 1 finely chopped shallot or ¼ cup (60 mL) finely chopped onion with the mushrooms.

Main Dishes

Chipotle Beef with Fresh Tomato Salsa

Makes 8 to 10 servings

Fresh cilantro, garlic and the unmistakable flavor of chipotle season beef brisket as it simmers all day. The fresh tomato salsa provides a flavor punch. This dish is a meal in itself!

Tip

Chipotle peppers are smoked jalapeño peppers and are often found canned in adobo sauce. Use one for this recipe, then freeze the rest in an airtight container for up to 6 months. For even more convenience, separate the peppers and place in a single layer on a tray, topped with a little adobo sauce; freeze until firm, then transfer each pepper to a sealable freezer bag. You can then use just the amount you need for each recipe.

Make Ahead

Prepare through step 1, cover and refrigerate overnight. Cook as directed.

1	onion, thinly sliced	1
2- to 2½-lb	beef brisket, well trimmed	1 to 1.25 kg
1	chipotle pepper in adobo sauce, chopped (see tip, at left)	1
1 tbsp	dry minced (granulated) garlic	15 mL
½ tsp	ground cumin	2 mL
½ tsp	salt	2 mL
½ cup	tomato juice	125 mL
¼ cup	minced fresh cilantro	60 mL
	Tomato Salsa (see recipe, opposite)	
	Flour tortillas, warmed	

1. Arrange onion slices in bottom of one slow cooker stoneware, overlapping as necessary. Cut brisket in half and place on top of onions. Sprinkle with chipotle pepper, garlic, cumin and salt. Pour tomato juice over top.

2. Cover and cook on Low for 9 to 11 hours or on High for 4½ to 5½ hours, until beef is very tender.

3. Using a slotted spoon, transfer beef and onions to a tray. Pour liquid into a deep bowl. Using two forks, shred beef. Return beef and onions to stoneware. Skim fat from liquid and pour over beef mixture. Sprinkle with cilantro. Turn to Warm for serving.

4. To serve, spoon beef mixture and salsa into center of each warm tortilla, then fold tortilla over filling.

It's so quick and easy to make your own salsa, and the fresh flavor just can't be captured in a jar. Give it a try.

Tip

If fresh tomatoes are not available, substitute a 14-oz (398 mL) can of diced tomatoes, drained.

Tomato Salsa

3	ripe tomatoes, seeded and chopped	3
2	green onions, sliced	2
1	jalapeño pepper, seeded and minced	1
2 tsp	minced fresh cilantro	10 mL
	Juice of 1 lime	
	Salt and freshly ground black pepper	

1. In a bowl, combine tomatoes, green onions, jalapeño, cilantro and lime juice. Season to taste with salt and pepper. Serve immediately or cover and refrigerate for up to 1 day.

Slow-Smoked Beef Brisket

Makes 15 to 20 servings

This is Roxanne's mother's signature dish. Roxanne has fond memories of her mom and dad entertaining. They usually served this brisket with twice-baked potatoes, green beans and her mom's famous Napoleon dessert.

Tip

If desired, you can cook the brisket in a 6-quart slow cooker instead of roasting it. Cut the brisket in half, season as directed and place the halves in the slow cooker. (Omit the foil wrap.) Cover and cook on Low for 8 to 10 hours or on High for 4 to 5 hours, until meat is fork-tender. Proceed with step 3.

- **Preheat oven to 500°F (260°C)**
- **Large roasting pan with 1½-inch (4 cm) sides**

8- to 10-lb	beef brisket, trimmed	4 to 4.5 kg
3 tbsp	seasoned salt	45 mL
6 to 8 tbsp	celery seed	90 to 125 mL
8	drops liquid smoke	8
	Barbecue sauce	

1. Place brisket in the center of a 30-inch (75 cm) piece of foil. Sprinkle one side with half each of the seasoned salt and celery seed. Rub into meat. Drizzle with 4 drops liquid smoke. Carefully turn brisket over and repeat process on second side. Top brisket with another 30-inch (75 cm) piece of foil and crimp all four sides tightly. Place in roasting pan.

2. Roast in preheated oven for 30 minutes. Without opening the oven door, reduce heat to 275°F (140°C) and roast for 4 to 5 hours or until beef is fork-tender.

3. Let cool slightly, then carefully remove foil. Transfer brisket to a large tray and let rest for 15 minutes. Reserve collected juices, if desired. Cut meat against the grain into thin slices. Fill one slow cooker stoneware about three-quarters full with meat slices (generally, this is about one-third of the meat) and top with barbecue sauce as desired. Cover and refrigerate the remaining meat.

4. Cover stoneware with plastic wrap and microwave on High for 5 to 7 minutes or until meat is steaming hot. Place stoneware in slow cooker, cover and cook on High for 30 minutes. Turn to Warm for serving.

Make Ahead

Roast the brisket through step 2. Let cool and carefully remove foil. Place meat on a large tray, cover tightly with plastic wrap and refrigerate. Cover and refrigerate collected juices separately. The next day, slice the meat and proceed with the recipe as directed in step 3. Increase the heating time for the collected juices to 3 to 4 minutes.

5. If you wish to serve the collected juices, pour them into a microwave-safe glass bowl. Skim off any fat. Cover and microwave on High for 2 to 3 minutes or until steaming hot. Serve alongside beef.

6. When more meat is needed, arrange about half the remaining slices in a microwave-safe dish. Cover with plastic wrap and microwave on High for 7 to 9 minutes or until hot, rearranging meat as necessary halfway through cooking so it is evenly hot. Transfer meat to stoneware and top with barbecue sauce. Cover and cook on High for 30 minutes. Repeat when the remaining meat is needed.

Beef Burgundy

Julia Child was a hero to both of us, and Roxanne had the incredible opportunity to travel to France with her! We like to serve this easy version of one of her most popular dishes — *boeuf Bourguignon* — any time we have a dinner party.

Tips

Sometimes we like to serve beef burgundy over hot cooked egg noodles or rice, other times over mashed potatoes.

Make sure to brown the beef in batches, leaving space between each piece. If you overfill the skillet, the beef will steam instead of browning.

5	slices bacon	5
2 tbsp	all-purpose flour	30 mL
½ tsp	salt	2 mL
¼ tsp	freshly ground black pepper	1 mL
2 to 2½ lbs	boneless beef chuck, blade or cross rib, cut into 1-inch (2.5 cm cubes) and patted dry	1 to 1.25 kg
	Vegetable oil	
½	onion, chopped	½
1 cup	sliced mushrooms	250 mL
12	pearl onions	12
1	carrot, sliced	1
1	bay leaf	1
2 tsp	dry minced (granulated) garlic	10 mL
½ tsp	dried thyme	2 mL
1 tbsp	tomato paste	15 mL
½ cup	reduced-sodium ready-to-use beef broth	125 mL
¼ cup	dry red wine	60 mL
1 tbsp	cornstarch	15 mL
2 tbsp	cold water	30 mL
2 tbsp	minced fresh parsley	30 mL

1. In a large skillet, cook bacon over medium heat until crisp. Transfer bacon to a plate lined with paper towels to drain. Reserve drippings in skillet.

2. In a large bowl or food-safe plastic bag, combine flour, salt and pepper. Add beef and toss to coat. Return skillet to medium-high heat and reheat drippings. Working in batches, cook beef, stirring often, for 6 to 8 minutes or until browned on all sides, adjusting heat and adding 1 to 2 tbsp (15 to 30 mL) oil as necessary between batches. Using a slotted spoon, transfer beef to one slow cooker stoneware. Discard any excess flour mixture.

Tips

Sautéing the chopped onions and sliced mushrooms adds depth of flavor to the finished dish, so it's worth the few minutes it takes.

Pearl onions are tiny, mildly flavored onions about the size of a marble. They are often sold in small bags in the produce section. Peel them and add them whole to the slow cooker.

Although it's not a traditional ingredient, you can add a diced peeled potato in step 4 if you prefer a more stew-like dish.

You can substitute a 4$\frac{1}{2}$-oz (140 g) can of whole mushrooms, drained, for the fresh mushrooms. Do not sauté them; simply add in step 4.

3. Add 2 tbsp (30 mL) oil to skillet. Add chopped onion and cook, stirring, for 2 to 3 minutes or until translucent. Add mushrooms and cook, stirring often, for 3 to 4 minutes or until onion and mushrooms are tender. Transfer to stoneware.

4. Crumble bacon and add to stoneware. Add pearl onions, carrot, bay leaf, garlic, thyme and tomato paste. Pour in broth and wine. Stir well.

5. Cover and cook on Low for 7 to 9 hours or on High for 3$\frac{1}{2}$ to 4$\frac{1}{2}$ hours, until beef and vegetables are tender. Discard bay leaf.

6. In a small bowl, stir together cornstarch and cold water to make a smooth paste. Stir into beef mixture. Cover and cook on High for 30 minutes, stirring halfway through. Stir in parsley. Turn to Warm for serving.

Easy Philly-Style Steak and Cheese Sandwiches

Makes 8 servings

Although our sandwiches aren't made with the traditional chipped and grilled beef, the flavor reminds us of Philly steak sandwiches. These are a great choice any time friends gather at your house.

Tips

If serving a larger crowd or if you want more modest servings, use small crusty French rolls, split and toasted.

For an even more traditional flavor, omit the provolone and spoon warmed processed cheese sauce or processed cheese spread over the meat on each sandwich.

For a flavor twist, add 1 tbsp (15 mL) dried Italian seasoning with the garlic.

Make Ahead

Prepare through step 1, cover and refrigerate overnight. Cook as directed.

1	onion, sliced	1
1	green bell pepper, sliced	1
2½- to 2¾-lb	boneless beef tri-tip, chuck pot roast or shoulder pot roast	1.25 to 1.4 kg
1 tbsp	dry minced (granulated) garlic	15 mL
½ tsp	freshly ground black pepper	2 mL
⅛ tsp	hot pepper flakes	0.5 mL
⅓ cup	reduced-sodium ready-to-use beef broth	75 mL
2 tbsp	reduced-sodium soy sauce	30 mL
2 tbsp	Worcestershire sauce	30 mL
	Salt	
	Hoagie rolls or crusty French rolls	
	Sliced provolone cheese	

1. Arrange onion and green pepper slices in bottom of one slow cooker stoneware, overlapping as necessary. Cut beef in half and place on top of vegetables. Sprinkle with garlic, black pepper and hot pepper flakes. Pour broth, soy sauce and Worcestershire sauce over top.

2. Cover and cook on Low for 8 to 10 hours or on High for 4 to 5 hours, until beef is very tender.

3. Using tongs, transfer beef to a cutting board, tent with foil and let rest for 5 to 10 minutes. Using a slotted spoon, transfer vegetables to a bowl and set aside. Pour liquid into a deep bowl and let cool slightly.

4. Thinly slice beef across the grain. Return beef and vegetables to stoneware. Skim fat from liquid. Season to taste with salt. Pour liquid over beef. Turn to Warm for serving.

5. Split rolls and toast lightly. To serve, top rolls with beef, vegetables and a piece of cheese.

Bourbon Barbecue Beef Sandwiches

Makes 6 to 8 servings

When Kathy's daughters came home from college, friends would gather and easy, casual food was in order. This was her "go-to" recipe. Everyone loved it, and it's so very easy to prepare.

Tips

Small cuts of beef are sometimes hard to find. Ask the butcher for help, or buy a larger roast and cut it in half. Use half for this recipe and freeze the other half in a freezer bag for use within about 9 months.

If you prefer a richer flavor (or if the meat is a little more fatty than desired), quickly brown the beef before slow cooking. Heat 2 tbsp (30 mL) vegetable oil in a large skillet. Add beef and cook, turning once, until well browned on both sides. Drain off accumulated fat. Proceed with step 1.

Make Ahead

Prepare through step 1, cover and refrigerate overnight. Cook as directed.

1	onion, sliced	1
2½- to 2¾-lb	boneless beef chuck or shoulder pot roast, blade or cross rib roast	1.25 to 1.4 kg
1 tbsp	dry minced (granulated) garlic	15 mL
½ tsp	salt	2 mL
½ tsp	freshly ground black pepper	2 mL
¼ cup	reduced-sodium ready-to-use beef broth	60 mL
¼ cup	bourbon	60 mL
1 cup	barbecue sauce	250 mL
	Hamburger buns, split and toasted	

1. Arrange onion slices in bottom of one slow cooker stoneware, overlapping as necessary. Cut roast in half and place on top of onions. Sprinkle with garlic, salt and pepper. Pour broth and bourbon over top.

2. Cover and cook on Low for 8 to 10 hours or on High for 4 to 5 hours, until beef is very tender.

3. Using tongs, transfer beef to a tray. Pour liquid into a deep bowl. Trim fat from beef. Using two forks, shred beef. Return beef to stoneware. Using a slotted spoon, lift onions from liquid and return to stoneware. Skim fat from liquid. Measure out ½ cup (125 mL) liquid and pour over beef (discard excess liquid). Stir in barbecue sauce.

4. Cover and cook on High for 30 minutes or until heated through. Turn to Warm for serving.

5. To serve, spoon beef and sauce onto buns.

Beef and Salsa Taco Filling

Makes 10 servings

This easy beef taco filling makes any Mexican fiesta fun and leaves plenty of extra time for you to enjoy a margarita. Use it to fill taco shells, enchiladas or quesadillas, fold it into warm flour tortillas or spoon it over a taco salad.

Tip

Top tacos with shredded lettuce, chopped tomatoes, chopped green onions, sour cream, guacamole and chopped pickled jalapeños, as desired.

Make Ahead

Brown beef, place in a shallow container and refrigerate until cold. Once it's chilled, proceed with step 3; cover and refrigerate overnight. Cook as directed.

	Nonstick baking spray	
2 lbs	lean ground beef	1 kg
½ cup	finely chopped onion	125 mL
1 tbsp	chili powder	15 mL
2 tsp	ground cumin	10 mL
1½ tsp	dry minced (granulated) garlic	7 mL
½ cup	salsa	125 mL

1. Spray one slow cooker stoneware with baking spray.

2. In a large skillet, cook beef over medium-high heat, breaking it up with a spoon and stirring often, for 6 to 8 minutes or until no longer pink. Drain off fat.

3. Transfer beef to one slow cooker stoneware. Stir in onion, chili powder, cumin, garlic and salsa.

4. Cover and cook on Low for 4 to 6 hours or on High for 2 to 3 hours, until hot. Turn to Warm for serving.

Slow-Roasted Cola Pork

Makes 10 to 12 servings

Roxanne enjoys cola immensely, but saves the indulgence for special occasions. What better way to enjoy it than in a delicious sauce for pork roast?

Make Ahead

Prepare through step 2, cover and refrigerate overnight. Cook as directed. Or, if serving as pulled pork, cook as directed and shred. Place in an airtight container and stir in ½ cup (125 mL) of the skimmed liquid. Cover and refrigerate. When ready to serve, transfer pork mixture to stoneware, cover with plastic wrap and microwave on High for 5 to 7 minutes, stirring halfway through, until steaming hot. Place stoneware in slow cooker. Cover and cook on High for 30 minutes. Turn to Warm for serving.

3-lb	boneless pork shoulder blade (butt) roast	1.5 kg
2 tbsp	packed brown sugar	30 mL
1 tsp	chili powder	5 mL
½ tsp	seasoned salt	2 mL
½ tsp	garlic powder	2 mL
½ cup	cola	125 mL
⅓ cup	ketchup	75 mL
2 tbsp	cider vinegar	30 mL
1 tbsp	Worcestershire sauce	15 mL

1. Spray one slow cooker stoneware with baking spray. Place pork in prepared stoneware.

2. In a small bowl, combine brown sugar, chili powder, seasoned salt, garlic powder, cola, ketchup, vinegar and Worcestershire sauce. Pour over pork.

3. Cover and cook on Low for 8 to 10 hours or on High for 4 to 5 hours, until pork is very tender.

4. Using tongs, transfer pork to a cutting board, tent with foil and let rest for 5 minutes. Pour liquid into a deep bowl. Trim fat from pork, then slice. Return pork to stoneware. Skim fat from liquid. Measure out ½ cup (125 mL) liquid and pour over pork (discard excess liquid). Turn to Warm for serving.

Pulled Pork Sandwiches

Remove pork from slow cooker, tent with foil and let rest for 5 minutes. Pour liquid into a deep bowl. Using two forks, shred pork, discarding fat. Return pork to stoneware. Skim fat from liquid. Measure out ½ cup (125 mL) liquid and pour over pork (discard excess liquid). Turn to Warm for serving. Serve on toasted buns.

Grilled Pork Tenderloin with Fig and Port Jam

Makes 8 to 10 servings

Elegant but easy! When Kathy served this at a dinner party on her patio, everyone loved it.

Tips

Pork tenderloin is a tender cut that cooks quickly. Do not overcook it, especially since it will continue to cook a bit once placed in the slow cooker.

Port is a red dessert wine. When combined with the onions and figs, it becomes a wonderful sauce for the pork.

Fig and Port Jam

8	dried Mission figs, chopped	8
2	sweet onions, chopped	2
¼ cup	packed brown sugar	60 mL
1 tsp	salt	5 mL
⅓ cup	port wine	75 mL
2 tbsp	red wine vinegar	30 mL

Grilled Pork Tenderloin

½ tsp	salt	2 mL
½ tsp	freshly ground black pepper	2 mL
½ tsp	dry mustard	2 mL
½ tsp	garlic powder	2 mL
2	pork tenderloins (each 1 to 1¼ lbs/500 to 625 g)	2
2 tbsp	olive oil	30 mL

1. *Jam:* In one slow cooker stoneware, combine figs, onions, brown sugar and salt. Stir in port and vinegar. Cover and cook on High for 5 to 6 hours or until onions are caramelized and juices form a thin syrup.

2. *Pork:* Preheat barbecue grill to medium. In a small bowl, combine salt, pepper, mustard and garlic powder. Brush tenderloins evenly and lightly with oil. Sprinkle evenly with seasoning mixture. Place on grill, close lid and grill, turning once, for about 20 minutes or until a meat thermometer inserted in the center of a tenderloin registers 145°F (63°C) and just a hint of pink remains in pork. Transfer to a cutting board, tent with foil and let rest for 5 minutes.

3. Slice pork into medallions about 1 inch (2.5 cm) thick. Add pork to stoneware, spooning jam over top. Cover and turn to Warm for serving.

Cajun Smoked Sausage Po' Boys

Makes 6 to 8 servings

Whenever we're in New Orleans we seek out a po' boy sandwich. Our take on the Crescent City classic makes a fun addition to a Mardi Gras party.

Tips

Select spicy sausage or smoked andouille if you enjoy spicy food.

If you like heat, add another teaspoon (5 mL) Cajun seasoning.

Toasting the buns helps prevents juices from seeping into them, keeping them crisp.

Make Ahead

Prepare through step 1, cover and refrigerate overnight. Cook as directed.

1	red or green bell pepper, halved lengthwise and thinly sliced	1
½	onion, thinly sliced	½
2	packages (each 14 oz/400 g) smoked sausages, cut into 1-inch (2.5 cm) pieces	2
2 tsp	chili powder	10 mL
1 tsp	Cajun seasoning	5 mL
1	can (14 oz/398 mL) diced tomatoes, with juice	1
1	can (10 oz/284 mL) diced tomatoes and green chiles, with juice	1
6 to 8	hoagie buns, split and lightly toasted	6 to 8

1. Arrange red pepper and onion slices in bottom of one slow cooker stoneware, overlapping as necessary. Place sausages on top of vegetables. Sprinkle with chili powder and Cajun seasoning. Top with tomatoes with juice and tomatoes and chiles with juice.

2. Cover and cook on Low for 4 to 6 hours or on High for 2 to 3 hours, until sausages are hot and sauce is bubbly. Turn to Warm for serving.

3. To serve, spoon sausages and vegetables onto each toasted bun.

Cuban Pork Sandwiches with Cilantro Mayonnaise

**Makes 8 to
10 servings**

These pork sandwiches
are just the ticket for any
casual gathering. The
Cilantro Mayonnaise
adds the crowning glory.

Tip

Make sure to toast the
buns — they'll stay crisper
when holding the warm,
juicy pork.

Make Ahead

Prepare through step 4,
refrigerating the shredded
pork and measured liquid in
separate airtight containers
for up to 1 day. When ready
to serve, combine pork
and liquid in stoneware,
cover with plastic wrap
and microwave on High
for 5 to 7 minutes, stirring
halfway through, until
pork is steaming hot. Place
stoneware in slow cooker.
Cover and cook on High for
30 minutes. Turn to Warm
for serving.

1	onion, sliced	1
2½- to 3-lb	boneless pork shoulder blade (butt) or sirloin roast	1.25 to 1.5 kg
1 tbsp	packed brown sugar	15 mL
2 tsp	dry minced (granulated) garlic	10 mL
1 tsp	ground cumin	5 mL
½ tsp	salt	2 mL
½ tsp	freshly ground black pepper	2 mL
	Juice of 1 lime	
¼ cup	water	60 mL
	Cilantro Mayonnaise (see recipe, opposite)	
8 to 10	hamburger buns, split and toasted	8 to 10

1. Arrange onion slices in bottom of one slow cooker stoneware, overlapping as necessary. Place pork roast on top of onions.

2. In a small bowl, combine brown sugar, garlic, cumin, salt and pepper. Sprinkle over pork. Pour lime juice and water around roast.

3. Cover and cook on Low for 8 to 10 hours or on High for 4 to 5 hours, until pork is very tender.

4. Transfer roast to a tray. Pour liquid into a deep bowl. Using two forks, shred pork, discarding fat. Return pork to stoneware. Skim fat from liquid. Measure out 1 cup (250 mL) liquid and pour over pork (discard excess liquid).

5. Cover and cook on High for 30 minutes or until heated through. Turn to Warm for serving.

6. To serve, spread Cilantro Mayonnaise on each bun. Top with pork.

This herb-spiked mayo makes an excellent spread for any sandwich, but is especially wonderful with Cuban Pork Sandwiches (opposite).

Cilantro Mayonnaise

1	clove garlic, minced	1
2 tbsp	minced fresh cilantro	30 mL
¹/₂ cup	mayonnaise	125 mL
1 tbsp	freshly squeezed lime juice	15 mL

1. In a small bowl, combine garlic, cilantro, mayonnaise and lime juice. Serve immediately or cover and refrigerate for up to 1 day.

Beer-Braised Brats

Makes 8 servings

Dads around the globe will enjoy these beer-flavored bratwurst sausages. We prepare them when it is too hot even to fire up the grill.

Tips

Roxanne's husband, Bob Bateman, adds some brats to the grill when he is preparing another meal, quickly searing them to add grill marks. Roxanne wraps and refrigerates the brats until later in the week, when she places them in the slow cooker to make this recipe for dinner.

We buy smoked brats at a local smokehouse/butcher and experiment with different flavors, from garlic to chile pepper to sun-dried tomato and basil. Many of these flavors are wonderful steeped in beer. Check your local stores to see if you can purchase such flavors.

Read the label to make sure the smoked brats you purchase are fully cooked.

8	fully cooked smoked bratwurst sausages	8
1 cup	beer	250 mL
½ tsp	dry minced (granulated) garlic	2 mL

1. Place bratwursts in one slow cooker stoneware. Add beer and garlic.
2. Cover and cook on Low for 4 to 6 hours or on High for 2 to 3 hours, until bratwursts are hot and sauce is bubbly. Turn to Warm for serving.

Kielbasa and Kraut

Makes 8 to 10 servings

On a wonderful vacation in Germany, sausages and kraut made a memorable dinner for Kathy, her husband, David, and their daughters. This dish carries them back to that little town in Bavaria.

Make Ahead

Prepare through step 1, cover and refrigerate overnight. Cook as directed.

2	packages (each 14 oz/400 g) kielbasa, cut into 1-inch (2.5 cm) pieces	2
½ cup	chopped onion	125 mL
1 tbsp	packed brown sugar	15 mL
½ tsp	fennel or caraway seeds	2 mL
¼ tsp	salt	1 mL
¼ tsp	freshly ground black pepper	1 mL
½ cup	reduced-sodium ready-to-use beef broth	125 mL
3 cups	sauerkraut, drained	750 mL

1. In one slow cooker stoneware, combine kielbasa, onion, brown sugar, fennel seeds, salt and pepper. Pour broth over top.

2. Cover and cook on Low for 4 to 5 hours or on High for 2 to 2½ hours, until kielbasa is hot and sauce is bubbly. Stir in sauerkraut. Cover and cook on High for 1 hour. Turn to Warm for serving.

Hot Dogs

Makes 16 to 20 servings

Slow-cooked hot dogs are the easiest and best, yet many people think they taste like those from the ball park.

Tip

With this convenient way to heat and serve hot dogs, you can be sure everyone's is hot. They stay warm for about 1 to 2 hours on Warm; any longer, and they may begin to split.

2	packages (each 16 oz/500 g) hot dog wieners	2
½ cup	water	125 mL
16 to 20	hot dog buns, split and toasted	16 to 20

1. Place wieners in one slow cooker stoneware. Pour in water.
2. Cover and cook on High for 1 to 2 hours or until heated through. Turn to Warm for serving.
3. Serve hot dogs on toasted buns.

Chicken con Queso

Makes 6 servings

Every Mexican buffet should include this fantastic chicken dish. Set out bowls of all of your favorite Mexican toppings — salsa, guacamole, sour cream, diced tomatoes and/ or additional shredded cheese.

Tips

The chicken con queso mixture is also very good on crisp tortilla chips and makes a terrific ready-made topping for nachos or filling for quesadillas or tostadas.

Adjust the amount of liquid you add back to the chicken mixture at the end of step 3 based on how thick you like the sauce.

Slow-cooking boneless skinless chicken breasts works well, but be careful not to overcook them. If you try to extend the cooking time, they will become dry.

1½ lbs	boneless skinless chicken breasts	750 g
1	jalapeño pepper, seeded and diced	1
1	clove garlic, minced	1
½ tsp	ground cumin	2 mL
¼ tsp	salt	1 mL
¼ tsp	freshly ground black pepper	1 mL
1 cup	reduced-sodium ready-to-use chicken broth	250 mL
1	can (4 oz/127 mL) chopped mild green chiles	1
1 cup	shredded Monterey Jack cheese	250 mL
2 tbsp	minced fresh cilantro	30 mL
½ cup	salsa	125 mL
¼ cup	sour cream	60 mL
	Flour tortillas, warmed	

1. Place chicken in one slow cooker stoneware. Sprinkle with jalapeño, garlic, cumin, salt and pepper. Pour broth over top.

2. Cover and cook on Low for 5 to 6 hours or on High for 2½ to 3 hours, until chicken is no longer pink inside and a meat thermometer inserted in the thickest part registers 165°F (74°C).

3. Using tongs, transfer chicken to a tray. Pour liquid into a deep bowl. Using two forks, shred chicken. Return chicken to stoneware and stir in green chiles, cheese, cilantro, salsa and sour cream. Skim fat from liquid. Measure out ½ cup (125 mL) liquid and pour into stoneware (discard excess liquid).

4. Cover and cook on Low for 30 minutes or until heated through. Turn to Warm for serving.

5. To serve, spoon chicken mixture into center of each warm tortilla, then fold tortilla over filling.

Hot Browns

Makes 8 to 10 servings

A hot brown is an open-face turkey sandwich first served at the Brown Hotel in Louisville, Kentucky, in the 1920s. People who gathered at the hotel for dances loved the new sandwich, and it became a classic. Any time you want a taste of the South, enjoy this Kentucky favorite.

Tip

Hot browns are traditionally broiled once the turkey in sauce is placed on the toast. This version is so good, it doesn't need to be broiled, but if you wish to, place the toast on a baking sheet and top with turkey in sauce. Broil until sauce begins to bubble and brown lightly. Top with tomatoes and bacon.

- Preheat oven to 325°F (160°C)
- Shallow roasting pan

Bourbon-Glazed Turkey

1	bone-in skin-on turkey breast (4½ to 5 lbs/2.25 to 2.5 kg)	1
½ tsp	dried thyme	2 mL
¼ tsp	garlic powder	1 mL
2 tbsp	unsalted butter, softened	30 mL
	Salt and freshly ground black pepper	
¼ cup	orange marmalade	60 mL
2 tbsp	bourbon	30 mL
1 tsp	Dijon mustard	5 mL

Mornay Sauce

3 tbsp	unsalted butter	30 mL
3 tbsp	all-purpose flour	30 mL
	Salt and freshly ground black pepper	
1 cup	reduced-sodium ready-to-use chicken broth	250 mL
½ cup	half-and-half (10%) cream	125 mL
½ cup	freshly grated Parmesan cheese	125 mL
½ cup	shredded Swiss cheese	125 mL

Sandwiches

8 to 10	slices bread, toasted	8 to 10
2	tomatoes, sliced	2
16 to 20	slices bacon, cooked crisp	16 to 20

1. *Turkey:* Place turkey breast, skin side up, in roasting pan. In a small bowl, combine thyme, garlic powder and butter. Season to taste with salt and pepper. Rub evenly over turkey.

2. Roast in preheated oven for 1½ to 2 hours or until a meat thermometer inserted in the thickest part registers about 150°F (70°C).

Make Ahead

Roast and carve turkey as directed. Place turkey slices in an airtight container and refrigerate overnight. When ready to serve, arrange turkey in stoneware, cover with plastic wrap and microwave on High for 5 to 7 minutes, rearranging turkey halfway through, until a meat thermometer inserted in the center registers 165°F (74°C). Proceed with step 5.

3. In a small bowl, combine marmalade, bourbon and mustard. Brush over turkey. Continue roasting until meat thermometer registers 165°F (74°C). Transfer turkey to a cutting board, tent with foil and let rest for 15 minutes.

4. Carve turkey, cutting slices about $\frac{1}{4}$ inch (0.5 cm) thick. Discard skin, if desired. Discard bones. Place turkey slices in one slow cooker stoneware.

5. *Sauce:* In a small saucepan, melt butter over medium heat. Stir in flour. Season to taste with salt and pepper. Cook, stirring constantly, for 1 minute. Gradually whisk in broth, then cream. Cook, stirring constantly, for about 5 minutes or until mixture bubbles and thickens. Stir in Parmesan and Swiss cheese; cook, stirring, just until cheese is melted. Pour over turkey.

6. Cover and cook on Low for 30 to 60 minutes or on High for 15 to 30 minutes, until turkey is hot and sauce is bubbly. Turn to Warm for serving.

7. *Sandwiches:* To serve, place each slice of toast on a plate. Top with turkey in sauce. Top with tomatoes and 2 slices of bacon.

New Orleans Spicy Barbecue Shrimp

**Makes 4 to
6 servings**

When people from
Kansas City say
"barbecue," they
usually mean ribs or
brisket. New Orleans,
on the other hand,
is known for its spicy
barbecued shrimp,
cooked with the shells
on to maximize flavor. To
serve in classic fashion,
cover the table with
newspaper and provide
plenty of napkins.

Tip

Shrimp sizes vary quite a lot
by the region, so our large
shrimp may not be the same
size as yours. This dish is
best with large to jumbo
shrimp, about 16 to 20 per
pound (500 g). If you have
smaller or larger shrimp,
adjust the cooking time as
needed so that they do not
overcook.

2	cloves garlic, minced	2
1 tsp	Cajun seasoning	5 mL
½ cup	unsalted butter, cut into pieces	125 mL
¼ cup	Worcestershire sauce	60 mL
1 tbsp	hot pepper sauce	15 mL
	Juice of 1 lemon	
	Salt and freshly ground black pepper	
1½ lbs	large shrimp (unpeeled)	750 g
1	green onion, finely chopped	1

1. In one slow cooker stoneware, combine garlic, Cajun seasoning, butter, Worcestershire sauce, hot pepper sauce and lemon juice. Season to taste with salt and pepper. Cover and cook on High for 30 minutes or until hot.

2. Rinse shrimp and drain. Spoon about half the sauce from the slow cooker into a heatproof measuring cup or bowl. Place shrimp in the sauce remaining in the stoneware. Drizzle with the reserved sauce. Stir to coat evenly.

3. Cover and cook on High for 30 minutes or until shrimp are pink, firm and opaque. Turn to Warm for serving. Sprinkle with green onion just before serving.

Sausage Hash Brown Casserole

Makes 8 to 10 servings

Many families gather for breakfast or brunch on holidays and special occasions. When it's your turn to host the party, serve this all-time favorite hash brown casserole.

Tip

Two kinds of frozen hash brown potatoes are commonly sold: shredded and Southern-style, which are more like nuggets. This recipe uses Southern-style.

	Nonstick baking spray	
8 oz	pork sausage (bulk or casings removed)	250 g
1½ lbs	frozen Southern-style hash brown potatoes	750 g
½	onion, finely chopped	½
½	red bell pepper, finely chopped	½
¼ cup	unsalted butter, melted	60 mL
	Salt and freshly ground black pepper	
4	large eggs, lightly beaten	4
2 cups	shredded Cheddar cheese, divided	500 mL

1. Spray one slow cooker stoneware with baking spray.

2. In a medium skillet, cook sausage over medium heat, breaking it up with a spoon and stirring often, for 5 to 7 minutes or until no longer pink. Drain off fat. Transfer sausage to a large bowl.

3. Stir potatoes into sausage. Stir in onion, red pepper and butter. Season to taste with salt and pepper. Spoon into prepared stoneware.

4. Cover and cook on High for 3 to 4 hours, stirring halfway through, until potatoes are tender. Stir in eggs and 1½ cups (375 mL) of the cheese. Cover and cook on High for 1 hour, stirring halfway through, until eggs are set. Sprinkle with the remaining cheese. Turn to Warm for serving.

Variations

Substitute Colby-Jack cheese for the Cheddar.

Add ⅛ to ¼ tsp (0.5 to 1 mL) hot pepper sauce with the butter.

Biscuits and Gravy

Makes 10 to 11 servings

Breakfast menus vary depending on family traditions and where you live — we are from biscuits and gravy country! Roxanne's mom made biscuits and gravy every weekend.

Tips

This makes biscuits and gravy for a crowd — or about 6 cups (1.5 L) of gravy. If serving fewer people, cut both the gravy and biscuit recipes in half.

For flaky biscuits, use very cold butter and shortening.

For tender biscuits, handle the dough lightly and do not overwork it. Lightly dust the work surface and rolling pin with flour; too much flour will make the biscuits heavy.

- 2-inch (5 cm) round biscuit cutter

Sausage Gravy

1 lb	pork sausage (bulk or casings removed)	500 g
2 tbsp	unsalted butter	30 mL
½ cup	all-purpose flour	125 mL
4 cups	milk	1 L
½ tsp	freshly ground black pepper (or to taste)	2 mL
Pinch	cayenne pepper	Pinch
	Salt	
	Nonstick baking spray	

Biscuits

3 cups	all-purpose flour	750 mL
4 tsp	baking powder	20 mL
1 tsp	baking soda	5 mL
½ tsp	salt	2 mL
⅓ cup	very cold unsalted butter, cut into pieces	75 mL
⅓ cup	very cold shortening	75 mL
1⅓ cups	buttermilk	325 mL

1. Spray one slow cooker stoneware with baking spray.

2. *Gravy:* In a large skillet, cook sausage over medium heat, breaking it up with a spoon and stirring often, for 6 to 8 minutes or until no longer pink. Do not drain. Stir in butter until melted. Stir in flour until smooth. Cook, stirring constantly, for 1 to 2 minutes or until evenly blended and flour is just starting to become golden brown. Gradually stir in about one-third of the milk. Cook, stirring constantly, until smooth and blended. Gradually stir in the remaining milk. Season with black pepper, cayenne and salt to taste. Pour into prepared stoneware.

3. Cover and cook on Low for 30 minutes. Turn to Warm for serving.

Dip the edge of the biscuit cutter in flour to prevent sticking.

Different sizes of biscuit cutters are available, so you can make slightly larger or smaller biscuits as you prefer. This will affect the yield and may affect the baking time. Keep checking on the biscuits while they're baking, and bake until golden brown.

4. *Biscuits:* Meanwhile, preheat oven to 450°F (230°C). In a large bowl, whisk together flour, baking powder, baking soda and salt. Using your fingertips or a pastry blender, cut in butter and shortening until mixture resembles coarse crumbs. Using a fork, stir in buttermilk just until dough comes together.

5. Turn dough out onto a lightly floured surface. Roll out to about $\frac{1}{2}$ inch (1 cm) thick. Using the biscuit cutter, cut 20 to 22 biscuits, rerolling scraps. Arrange at least 1 inch (2.5 cm) apart on a baking sheet.

6. Bake for 10 to 12 minutes or until golden brown.

7. To serve, split warm biscuits in half and spoon gravy over top.

Variation

Substitute link breakfast sausages for the bulk sausage. Slice the sausages into bite-size pieces, about $\frac{1}{2}$ inch (1 cm) long, brown them in a large skillet, then continue with step 2, stirring in butter and flour and proceeding as directed.

Overnight Fruited Oatmeal

Makes 8 to 10 servings

So healthy and so very warm and comforting, this wonderful oatmeal cooks slowly while you sleep.

Tips

If you prefer, you can omit the apple juice and use 6 cups (1.5 L) water.

Toasting walnuts intensifies their flavor. Spread chopped walnuts in a single layer on a baking sheet. Bake at 350°F (180°C) for 5 to 7 minutes or until lightly browned. Let cool.

	Nonstick baking spray	
1½ cups	steel-cut oats	375 mL
⅓ cup	raisins	75 mL
1 tsp	ground cinnamon	5 mL
4 cups	water	1 L
2 cups	unsweetened apple juice	500 mL
⅓ cup	chopped walnuts, toasted (see tip, at left)	75 mL

1. Spray one slow cooker stoneware with baking spray. Add oats, raisins, cinnamon, water and apple juice, stirring to combine.

2. Cover and cook on Low for 6 to 8 hours or until thick. Turn to Warm for serving.

3. To serve, spoon oatmeal into bowls and sprinkle with walnuts.

Sides and Salads

Savory Sage Bread Dressing

Makes 12 to 14 servings

For us, dressing is the star of the holiday feast, especially when it's packed with flavor and tradition, like this one. We make it every year.

Tips

Do you like your dressing moist or dry? We love it both ways. Adjust the amount of broth based on your preference. Stir in 1 cup (250 mL) broth, then add more if you prefer a moister dressing. Remember, the dressing will not dry out as it might in the oven.

If you like a strong herb flavor, double the poultry seasoning, sage and thyme in this dish.

Make Ahead

Bake the bread cubes the day before. Let stand at room temperature overnight so they are very dry the next day.

● **Preheat oven to 300°F (150°C)**

	Nonstick baking spray	
1 lb	firmly textured white bread, cut into ¾-inch (2 cm) cubes	500 g
¼ cup	unsalted butter	60 mL
2	stalks celery, finely chopped	2
1	large onion, finely chopped	1
1¼ cups	sliced mushrooms	300 mL
1 tsp	poultry seasoning	5 mL
1 tsp	dried rubbed sage	5 mL
¼ tsp	dried thyme	1 mL
	Salt and freshly ground black pepper	
1	large egg, lightly beaten	1
1 to 1¼ cups	reduced-sodium ready-to-use chicken broth	250 to 300 mL

1. Spray one slow cooker stoneware with baking spray.

2. Arrange bread cubes on a baking sheet. Bake in preheated oven for 30 minutes or until dry. Let cool on pan on a wire rack. Transfer to a large bowl.

3. In a large skillet, melt butter over medium-high heat. Add celery, onion and mushrooms; cook, stirring often, for about 5 minutes or until onion is tender. Add to bread cubes, along with poultry seasoning, sage and thyme. Season to taste with salt and pepper. Stir in egg. Add just enough of the broth to moisten to desired consistency (see tip, at left). Spoon into prepared stoneware.

4. Cover and cook on Low for 5 to 6 hours or on High for 2½ to 3 hours, until hot. Turn to Warm for serving.

Mashed Potatoes

Makes 14 to
16 servings

Perhaps the biggest
challenge for a holiday
feast is how to keep the
mashed potatoes hot
while avoiding a last-
minute rush. This recipe
to the rescue!

Make Ahead

Prepare through step 3,
cover and refrigerate
overnight. When ready to
cook, let stand at room
temperature for 30 minutes.
Cook on High for 3 to
4 hours, stirring once every
hour, until hot.

	Nonstick baking spray	
4 lbs	oblong baking potatoes (such as russet), peeled and cut into 1-inch (2.5 cm) cubes	2 kg
	Salt	
½ cup	unsalted butter, softened	125 mL
8 oz	cream cheese, softened and cut into pieces	250 g
½ cup	milk	125 mL
⅓ cup	sour cream	75 mL
1 tsp	seasoned salt	5 mL
	Freshly ground black pepper	

1. Spray one slow cooker stoneware with baking spray.

2. Place potatoes in a large saucepan and cover with cold water. Season with salt. Bring to a boil over medium-high heat. Reduce heat and boil gently for 20 to 30 minutes or until potatoes are very tender. Drain and return potatoes to pan. Heat over low heat, stirring, for 1 minute or until any remaining liquid has evaporated.

3. Add butter and cream cheese; mash potatoes until smooth. Stir in milk, sour cream, seasoned salt and pepper to taste. Transfer to prepared stoneware.

4. Cover and cook on High for 2 to 3 hours, stirring once every hour, until hot. Turn to Warm for serving.

Variation

Parmesan Mashed Potatoes: Stir in ¾ cup (175 mL) freshly grated Parmesan cheese with the sour cream.

Parmesan Herb Potato Casserole

Makes 10 to 12 servings

Convenience never tasted so good. Begin with frozen hash brown potatoes, then transform them into a culinary delight.

Tip

Two kinds of frozen hash brown potatoes are commonly sold: shredded and Southern-style, which are more like nuggets. This recipe uses Southern-style. Thaw the potatoes at room temperature for about 30 minutes so they easily break apart.

The stoneware will be quite full when you first spoon the potato mixture into it, so press the mixture down lightly with the back of a spoon. The casserole will shrink down once it begins to cook, but be sure the lid is flat on the appliance at the start.

Make Ahead

Prepare through step 2, cover and refrigerate overnight. Cook as directed.

	Nonstick baking spray	
½ cup	finely chopped onion	125 mL
1 tsp	salt	5 mL
1 tsp	garlic powder	5 mL
½ tsp	freshly ground black pepper	2 mL
½ tsp	dried thyme	2 mL
1	can (10 oz/284 mL) condensed cream of chicken soup	1
¾ cup	sour cream	175 mL
⅔ cup	milk	150 mL
¼ cup	unsalted butter, melted	60 mL
2 lbs	frozen Southern-style hash brown potatoes, partially thawed	1 kg
2 cups	shredded Cheddar cheese, divided	500 mL
¾ cup	freshly grated Parmesan cheese, divided	175 mL
2 tbsp	minced fresh parsley	30 mL

1. Spray one slow cooker stoneware with baking spray.

2. In a large bowl, combine onion, salt, garlic powder, pepper, thyme, soup, sour cream, milk and butter. Stir in potatoes, 1½ cups (375 mL) of the Cheddar and ½ cup (125 mL) of the Parmesan. Transfer to prepared stoneware (see tip, at left).

3. Cover and cook on High for 3 to 4 hours, stirring halfway through, until hot and bubbly.

4. Sprinkle with parsley and the remaining Cheddar and Parmesan. Cover and cook on Low for 15 minutes or until cheese is melted. Turn to Warm for serving.

German Potato Salad

Makes 8 to 10 servings

On a trip to central Germany, Kathy's family enjoyed lunch at a delightful restaurant that served a potato salad with a mild vinegar dressing. Like theirs, our slow cooker version has a milder vinegar flavor than other German potato salads you may have had, but we love it, and we think you will too!

Tip

Feel free to substitute cider vinegar for the white wine vinegar if you prefer. If you like a stronger vinegar flavor, increase the vinegar to 1/2 cup (125 mL).

Make Ahead

Prepare through step 2, place potatoes in an airtight container and refrigerate. Cook bacon, crumble and refrigerate in an airtight container. Prepare the onion mixture as directed in step 4, stirring in the salt, pepper and vinegar, but do not pour over the potatoes. Transfer dressing to an airtight container and refrigerate. The next day, place potatoes and bacon in the stoneware and drizzle with dressing. Cook as directed.

3 lbs	oblong baking potatoes, such as russet (about 8 medium)	1.5 kg
	Salt	
8	slices bacon	8
1	onion, chopped	1
3/4 cup	reduced-sodium ready-to-use beef broth	175 mL
1/2 tsp	salt	2 mL
1/4 tsp	freshly ground black pepper	1 mL
1/3 cup	white wine vinegar	75 mL
2 tbsp	minced fresh parsley	30 mL

1. Place potatoes in a large saucepan and cover with cold water. Season with salt. Bring to a boil over medium-high heat. Reduce heat and boil gently for 13 to 15 minutes or until potatoes can be pierced with a fork but are not overly tender. Drain and let cool slightly.

2. When cool enough to handle, peel potatoes and cut crosswise into 1/2-inch (1 cm) thick slices. Place potato slices in one slow cooker stoneware.

3. In a large skillet, cook bacon over medium heat until crisp. Transfer bacon to a plate lined with paper towels to drain. Reserve drippings in skillet.

4. Add onion to skillet and cook, stirring often, for 3 minutes or until translucent. Stir in broth and bring to a boil. Remove from heat and stir in salt, pepper and vinegar. Pour over potatoes. Crumble bacon and sprinkle over potatoes. Toss gently.

5. Cover and cook on Low for 4 to 6 hours or on High for 2 to 3 hours, until potatoes are as tender as desired. Sprinkle with parsley. Turn to Warm for serving.

Roasted Sweet Potatoes

Makes 12 servings

Thanksgiving wouldn't be complete without sweet potatoes, but maybe it's time to retire that old-fashioned recipe. This one is so good it will become an instant favorite that you'll serve year-round.

Tips

Sprinkle with toasted chopped walnuts and minced fresh sage just before serving.

Sweet potatoes discolor rapidly once peeled, but the orange juice mixture helps protect their color. Be sure all of the sweet potatoes are evenly coated.

1½ to 2 lbs	sweet potatoes (4 to 5 medium), peeled	750 g to 1 kg
2	cloves garlic, minced	2
2 tbsp	minced fresh sage	30 mL
	Salt and freshly ground black pepper	
¼ cup	orange juice	60 mL
2 tbsp	olive oil	30 mL
¾ cup	packed brown sugar	175 mL
¼ cup	water	60 mL
2 tbsp	white wine vinegar	30 mL

1. Cut sweet potatoes in half lengthwise, then cut each half crosswise into ½-inch (1 cm) thick slices.

2. In a large bowl or sealable plastic bag, toss together sweet potatoes, garlic, sage, salt and pepper to taste, orange juice and oil until sweet potatoes are evenly coated. Transfer to one slow cooker stoneware.

3. In a small microwave-safe bowl, combine brown sugar and water. Microwave on High for 1½ minutes or until boiling. Stir in vinegar. Drizzle over potato mixture.

4. Cover and cook on High for 4 to 5 hours, until sweet potatoes are tender. Turn to Warm for serving.

Family Favorite Macaroni and Cheese

Makes 8 to 10 servings

This version of the all-time favorite for kids of all ages is so very easy. For a lively flavor twist, try the Tex-Mex variation.

	Nonstick baking spray	
1	jar (15 oz or 500 g) processed cheese sauce or spread (such as Cheez Whiz)	1
1	can (12 oz or 370 mL) evaporated milk	1
2 cups	water	500 mL
1 tbsp	unsalted butter	15 mL
½ tsp	salt	2 mL
3 cups	shredded Cheddar-Jack or Cheddar cheese	750 mL
12 oz	uncooked elbow macaroni	375 g

1. Spray one slow cooker stoneware with baking spray.

2. In a medium saucepan, combine cheese sauce, milk, water, butter and salt. Bring to a simmer over medium heat, stirring often. Stir in cheese until melted. Remove from heat and stir in macaroni. Transfer to prepared stoneware.

3. Cover and cook on High for 2 hours or until sauce is bubbly and macaroni is tender. Turn to Warm for serving.

Variation

Tex-Mex Macaroni and Cheese: Substitute a 15-oz (500 mL) jar of salsa con queso or jalapeño Tex-Mex-flavored cheese spread for the processed cheese sauce, and substitute a shredded Mexican cheese blend for the Cheddar-Jack. Stir in a 4-oz (127 mL) can of chopped mild green chiles with the shredded cheese.

Bacon Macaroni and Cheese

Makes 8 to 10 servings

Roxanne's daughter, Grace, has loved macaroni and cheese since she was a toddler. This slow cooker recipe is so easy, Roxanne has no problem with making it often.

Tip

This version of mac and cheese also tastes good without the bacon.

	Nonstick baking spray	
2	cans (each 10 oz/284 mL) condensed Cheddar cheese soup	2
1	can (12 oz or 370 mL) evaporated milk	1
1½ cups	water	375 mL
3 cups	shredded sharp (old) Cheddar cheese (about 12 oz/375 g)	750 mL
½ tsp	salt	2 mL
12 oz	uncooked elbow macaroni	375 g
6 tbsp	cooked bacon pieces (about 9 slices, cooked crisp and crumbled)	90 mL

1. Spray one slow cooker stoneware with baking spray.

2. In a medium saucepan, combine soup, milk and water. Bring to a simmer over medium heat, stirring often. Stir in cheese and salt until cheese is melted. Remove from heat and stir in macaroni and bacon pieces. Transfer to prepared stoneware.

3. Cover and cook on High for 2 hours or until sauce is bubbly and macaroni is tender. Turn to Warm for serving.

Creamy Parmesan Polenta

Makes 10 servings

Tired of potatoes and rice? Try polenta. This easy slow cooker recipe means no last-minute rush.

Tips

We love to top polenta with Caramelized Onions (page 158).

For a great first course or meatless main dish, serve the vegetables from the Caponata Crostini (page 94) with this polenta.

	Nonstick baking spray	
1 cup	coarsely ground cornmeal or polenta	250 mL
½ tsp	salt (or to taste)	2 mL
½ tsp	freshly ground black pepper	2 mL
4 cups	reduced-sodium ready-to-use chicken broth	1 L
¼ cup	unsalted butter	60 mL
¾ cup	freshly grated Parmesan cheese	175 mL
½ cup	half-and-half (10%) cream	125 mL

1. Spray one slow cooker stoneware with baking spray.

2. In a medium saucepan, whisk together cornmeal, salt, pepper, broth and butter. Bring to a boil over medium-high heat, whisking constantly. Boil, whisking constantly, for 1 minute. Transfer to prepared stoneware.

3. Cover and cook on High for 2 hours, stirring every 30 minutes. Stir in Parmesan and cream. Cover and cook on Low for 30 minutes or until hot and cheese is melted. Turn to Warm for serving.

Herbed Rice Pilaf

Makes 10 servings

The irresistible flavor combination of brown and white rice makes this the ideal side dish for any dinner party. Sautéing the rice in butter before slow cooking ensures that the kernels stay more separate, so it doesn't get sticky.

Tips

Season the pilaf with an herb that complements your main dish. For example, substitute sage for the thyme if serving a pork or turkey dish, or use basil or tarragon if serving an Italian- or French-inspired chicken dish.

For best results, assemble this recipe just before cooking.

Parboiled rice, such as Uncle Ben's Converted Rice, has been through a steam process. It is often preferred for slow cooking as the grains stay separate and do not overcook as easily during the long cooking time.

3 tbsp	unsalted butter	45 mL
1/4 cup	chopped onion	60 mL
1	clove garlic, minced	1
3/4 cup	parboiled (Converted) long-grain white rice	175 mL
1/2 cup	long-grain brown rice	125 mL
1/2 tsp	dried thyme	2 mL
1/2 tsp	salt	2 mL
1/4 tsp	freshly ground black pepper	1 mL
1 3/4 cups	reduced-sodium ready-to-use chicken broth	425 mL
1 cup	water	250 mL
2 tbsp	minced fresh parsley	30 mL

1. In a large skillet, melt butter over medium-high heat. Add onion and garlic; cook, stirring often, for 3 to 4 minutes or until onion is tender-crisp. Stir in white rice and brown rice; cook, stirring often, for 3 minutes or until rice is golden brown.

2. Transfer rice mixture to one slow cooker stoneware. Stir in thyme, salt, pepper, broth and water.

3. Cover and cook on Low for 5 to 7 hours or until liquid is absorbed and rice is tender. Turn to Warm for serving. Stir in parsley just before serving.

Spanish Rice

Makes 8 to 10 servings

Spanish rice is actually seasoned with flavors often associated with Mexican or Tex-Mex dishes. Serve this side dish with Beef and Salsa Taco Filling (page 124), Chipotle Beef (page 116) or any other Mexican entrée.

Tips

Parboiled rice, such as Uncle Ben's Converted Rice, has been through a steam process. It is often preferred for slow cooking as the grains stay separate and do not overcook as easily during the long cooking time.

For best results, assemble this recipe just before cooking.

3 tbsp	olive oil	45 mL
½ cup	chopped onion	125 mL
½ cup	chopped green bell pepper	125 mL
2	cloves garlic, minced	2
1¼ cups	parboiled (Converted) long-grain white rice	300 mL
2 tsp	chili powder	10 mL
1	can (14 oz/398 mL) diced tomatoes, with juice	1
½ cup	picante sauce or salsa	125 mL
½ cup	water	125 mL

1. In a large skillet, heat oil over medium-high heat. Add onion, green pepper and garlic; cook, stirring often, for 3 minutes or until tender-crisp. Stir in rice and cook, stirring often, for 3 minutes or until rice is golden brown.

2. Transfer to one slow cooker stoneware. Stir in chili powder, tomatoes with juice, picante sauce and water.

3. Cover and cook on Low for 5 to 7 hours or until liquid is absorbed and rice is tender. Turn to Warm for serving.

Red Beans and Rice

Makes 6 to 8 servings

This New Orleans classic makes a perfect side dish for any Mardi Gras party.

Tips

Use andouille if you like traditional New Orleans flavors or spicy food.

If you wish to use dried beans instead of canned, sort and rinse 8 oz (250 g) red beans. Place beans in a large bowl, cover with water and soak overnight. Drain. Place beans in a large saucepan and add fresh water to cover. Bring to a boil over high heat. Boil for 10 minutes; drain. Add beans to stoneware as directed in step 2, and add 1 cup (250 mL) water. Cover and cook on High for 2 hours, then on Low for 5 to 7 hours, until beans are tender. Proceed with step 4.

1 tbsp	vegetable oil	15 mL
½	onion, chopped	½
¼ cup	chopped celery	60 mL
4 oz	smoked andouille or spicy sausage, finely chopped	125 g
2	cans (each 14 to 19 oz/398 to 540 mL) kidney beans, drained and rinsed	2
1	bay leaf	1
2 tsp	dry minced (granulated) garlic	10 mL
1 tsp	Cajun seasoning	5 mL
¼ tsp	cayenne pepper	1 mL
1¾ cups	reduced-sodium ready-to-use chicken broth	425 mL
½	green bell pepper, chopped	½
½ cup	parboiled (Converted) long-grain white rice	125 mL

1. In a medium skillet, heat oil over medium heat. Add onion and celery; cook, stirring often, for 2 to 3 minutes or until onion is translucent. Add sausage and cook, stirring often, for 3 to 4 minutes or until onion is tender and sausage is lightly browned.

2. Transfer sausage mixture to one slow cooker stoneware. Stir in beans, bay leaf, garlic, Cajun seasoning, cayenne and broth.

3. Cover and cook on Low for 5 to 7 hours or on High for 2 to 3 hours, until hot and bubbly.

4. Discard bay leaf. Stir in green pepper and rice. Cover and cook on High for 1 hour or until rice is tender. Turn to Warm for serving.

Cuban-Style Black Beans

Makes 8 to 10 servings

A great Latin flavor enhances the earthy goodness of black beans in this dish. We often serve it with Cuban Pork Sandwiches with Cilantro Mayonnaise (page 128).

Tip

For spicier beans, increase the hot pepper sauce to 1/2 tsp (2 mL).

Make Ahead

Prepare through step 2, cover and refrigerate overnight. Cook as directed.

2 tbsp	vegetable oil	30 mL
1	large green bell pepper, finely chopped	1
1	onion, finely chopped	1
3	cloves garlic, minced	3
2	cans (each 14 to 19 oz/398 to 540 mL) black beans, drained and rinsed	2
1	can (14 oz/398 mL) diced tomatoes, with juice	1
2	bay leaves	2
1 tbsp	ground cumin	15 mL
1 tbsp	chili powder	15 mL
1 tsp	dried oregano	5 mL
1/2 tsp	salt	2 mL
1/4 tsp	freshly ground black pepper	1 mL
1/4 tsp	hot pepper sauce	1 mL
3 tbsp	snipped fresh cilantro	45 mL
1/3 cup	chopped red onion	75 mL
	Hot cooked rice	

1. In a medium skillet, heat oil over medium heat. Add green pepper, finely chopped onion and garlic; cook, stirring often, for about 5 minutes or until onion is tender.

2. Transfer onion mixture to one slow cooker stoneware. Stir in beans, tomatoes with juice, bay leaves, cumin, chili powder, oregano, salt, black pepper and hot pepper sauce.

3. Cover and cook on Low for 4 to 6 hours or on High for 2 to 3 hours, until hot and bubbly. Discard bay leaves. Turn to Warm for serving. Sprinkle with cilantro and red onion just before serving. Serve over rice.

Old-Fashioned Baked Beans

Makes 10 to 12 servings

This classic side dish is a great choice for a backyard barbecue.

Tips

If you can't find a 53-oz (1.5 kg) can of pork and beans, use 3 or 4 smaller cans, or about 11⅓ cups (2.825 L).

Check on the beans 30 minutes before the end of cooking. If there's too much liquid, remove the lid for the remainder of the cooking time.

Make Ahead

Prepare through step 2, cover and refrigerate overnight. Cook as directed.

	Nonstick baking spray	
¼ cup	packed brown sugar	60 mL
2 tbsp	dry minced onion	30 mL
1	can (53 oz/1.5 L) pork and beans, with liquid partially drained	1
½ cup	ketchup	125 mL
¼ cup	light (fancy) molasses	60 mL
2 tbsp	prepared mustard	30 mL
½ tsp	hot pepper sauce	2 mL

1. Spray one slow cooker stoneware with baking spray.

2. In a medium bowl, combine brown sugar, onion, pork and beans, ketchup, molasses, mustard and hot pepper sauce. Transfer to one slow cooker stoneware.

3. Cover and cook on Low for 4 to 6 hours or on High for 2 to 3 hours, until hot and bubbly. Turn to Warm for serving.

Variation

Add 4 slices of bacon, cooked crisp and crumbled, with the beans.

Slow-Simmered Pinto Beans

**Makes 6 to
8 servings**

Each of us has had the
opportunity to work
with wonderful mentors
during our careers. This
recipe was inspired by
Roxanne's Texan mentor
and dear friend, Pat
Pitman Smith.

Tips

If a thicker texture is desired,
just before serving remove
some of the beans, mash
with a fork and return to the
stoneware.

Serve this as a side dish with
tacos and enchiladas, or with
cornbread as a main dish.

Make Ahead

Prepare through step 1,
cover and refrigerate
overnight. Cook as directed.

3	cans (each 14 to 19 oz/ 398 to 540 mL) pinto beans, drained and rinsed	3
1 cup	chopped cooked ham	250 mL
2 tsp	chili powder	10 mL
½ tsp	ground cumin	2 mL
¼ tsp	garlic powder	1 mL
½ cup	salsa	125 mL
1 tbsp	Worcestershire sauce	15 mL
	Salt and freshly ground black pepper	

1. Place beans in one slow cooker stoneware. Stir in
   ham, chili powder, cumin, garlic powder, salsa and
   Worcestershire sauce. Season to taste with salt and
   pepper.

2. Cover and cook on Low for 4 to 5 hours or on High for
   2 to 2½ hours, until hot and bubbly. Turn to Warm for
   serving.

Classic Green Bean Casserole

**Makes 14 to
16 servings**

This traditional side dish completes almost any meal.

Make Ahead

Prepare through step 3, cover and refrigerate overnight. Proceed with step 4, but reduce the cooking time to 3 to 5 hours.

	Nonstick baking spray	
2 tbsp	unsalted butter	30 mL
¼ cup	chopped onion	60 mL
1	clove garlic, minced	1
2 lbs	frozen cut green beans	1 kg
2 cups	shredded Cheddar cheese, divided	500 mL
1	jar (2 oz/60 mL) pimentos, drained	1
1	can (10 oz/284 mL) condensed cream of mushroom soup	1
	Salt and freshly ground black pepper	
1½ cups	canned french-fried onion rings	375 mL

1. Spray one slow cooker stoneware with baking spray.

2. In a medium skillet, melt butter over medium-high heat. Add chopped onion and garlic; cook, stirring often, for 3 to 4 minutes or until onion is tender.

3. Transfer onion mixture to a large bowl. Stir in green beans, 1 cup (250 mL) of the cheese, pimientos and soup. Season to taste with salt and pepper. Spoon into prepared stoneware.

4. Cover and cook on High for 4 to 6 hours or until beans are tender and sauce is bubbly. Turn to Warm for serving. Just before serving, stir in the remaining cheese and sprinkle top with onion rings.

Variation

Add 1 cup (250 mL) sliced mushrooms with the chopped onion and increase the cooking time in step 2 to 4 to 5 minutes.

Tangy Red Cabbage

**Makes 6 to
8 servings**

Kathy's and Roxanne's families have enjoyed several trips to the Amana colonies in Amana, Iowa. No such trip is complete without sampling the German fare served at many of the local restaurants. Roxanne always orders schnitzel with red cabbage, and we developed this recipe so that she could recreate the experience at home.

Tip

Serve this alongside Beer-Braised Brats (page 130).

½	head red cabbage, thinly sliced	½
1	red onion, chopped	1
1	tart apple, peeled and diced	1
2 tbsp	packed brown sugar	30 mL
½ tsp	salt	2 mL
3 tbsp	cider vinegar	45 mL
2 tbsp	water	30 mL

1. In one slow cooker stoneware, combine cabbage, red onion, apple, brown sugar, salt, vinegar and water.

2. Cover and cook on Low for 5 to 7 hours or on High for 2½ to 3½ hours, until cabbage is tender. Turn to Warm for serving.

Caramelized Onions

Makes about 3½ cups (875 mL)

Caramelized onions add a flavor punch to so many recipes. Use them for Mushroom and Caramelized Onion Bruschetta (page 92) or to top any of your favorite sandwiches, pizzas or meats.

Tip

Keep a supply of caramelized onions in the freezer, ready to use any time you need them. Spoon ½- to 1-cup (125 to 250 mL) portions of caramelized onions into small airtight containers and freeze for up to 6 months. Set a container in the refrigerator to thaw the night before you plan to use it.

4 to 5	sweet onions (see tip, page 98), thinly sliced	4 to 5
2 tbsp	olive oil	30 mL
2 tbsp	unsalted butter, cut into pieces	30 mL
	Salt and freshly ground black pepper	

1. In one slow cooker stoneware, combine onions, oil and butter.

2. Cover and cook on High for 6 to 8 hours. Season to taste with salt and pepper.

Old-Fashioned Warm Fruit Compote

Makes 6 to 8 servings

This fruit compote combines old-fashioned ease with trendy flavor thanks to the wide variety of dried fruits on the market today.

Tip

Select a combination of dried fruits, such as apricots, peaches, apples, berries, plums and cherries. Cut larger pieces of fruit into quarters.

3 cups	chopped dried fruits (see tip, at left)	750 mL
1/4 cup	granulated sugar	60 mL
1	2- to 3-inch (5 to 7.5 cm) cinnamon stick	1
1 tsp	minced crystallized ginger	5 mL
2 cups	water	500 mL
1/2 cup	orange juice	125 mL

1. In one slow cooker stoneware, combine dried fruits and sugar. Stir in cinnamon stick, ginger, water and orange juice.

2. Cover and cook on Low for 6 to 7 hours or on High for 3 to 3 1/2 hours, until bubbly and fruit is tender. Discard cinnamon stick. Turn to Warm for serving.

Strawberry Spinach Salad

Makes 6 servings

We have both had this salad in our recipe files for years. We can no longer remember who made it first, but one of us shared it with the other and now we both make it often.

Tips

Adjust the amount of spinach as desired if you need a larger or smaller salad.

You can sub in other fresh salad greens for some of the spinach.

Toasting almonds intensifies their flavor. Spread sliced almonds in a single layer on a baking sheet. Bake at 350°F (180°C) for 5 to 7 minutes or until lightly browned. Let cool.

To hard-cook eggs, place them in a single layer in a medium saucepan. Add enough cold water to cover by 1 inch (2.5 cm). Bring to a boil over medium-high heat. Remove from heat, cover and let stand for 12 minutes (for large eggs). Drain and rinse with cool water. Peel.

Make Ahead

Prepare the dressing, cover and refrigerate overnight. Wait to dress the salad until just before serving.

- Blender or food processor

Salad

6 cups	fresh spinach, stems trimmed	1.5 L
1 cup	strawberries, hulled and sliced	250 mL
1	red onion, cut into thin slivers	1
1/4 cup	sliced almonds, toasted (see tip, at left)	60 mL
1 to 2	hard-cooked eggs, sliced	1 to 2

Poppy Seed Dressing

1/4 cup	granulated sugar	60 mL
1/4 tsp	paprika	1 mL
1/2 cup	vegetable oil	125 mL
1/4 cup	cider vinegar	60 mL
1/2 tsp	Worcestershire sauce	2 mL
1 tbsp	poppy seeds	15 mL

1. *Salad:* In a large bowl, toss together spinach, strawberries and red onion. Toss in almonds and egg slices to taste.

2. *Dressing:* In blender, combine sugar, paprika, oil, vinegar and Worcestershire sauce; pulse to blend. Pour into a glass carafe and stir in poppy seeds.

3. Just before serving, drizzle salad with dressing.

Winter Salad

Makes 6 servings

This is our absolute favorite salad — and not just in the winter. The dressing is fantastic no matter what combination of greens you choose. The addition of walnuts, cranberries and goat cheese makes it perfect.

Tips

Adjust the amount of salad greens as desired if you need a larger or smaller salad.

When we teach cooking classes, Roxanne always mentions that she soaks greens in a sink full of ice water, then places the wet greens in a clean pillowcase (reserved for food), goes outside and swings the bag. This tip always gets a laugh, but it really is a great way to dry the greens. Crisp and dry greens make the very best salads.

Make Ahead

Prepare the dressing, cover and refrigerate overnight. Bring to room temperature and whisk well before use. Wait to dress the salad until just before serving.

Salad

6 cups	salad greens (such as spring mix with arugula)	1.5 L
2	slices bacon, cooked crisp and crumbled	2
3 tbsp	sweetened dried cranberries	45 mL
¼ cup	crumbled goat cheese	60 mL
3 tbsp	coarsely chopped walnuts, toasted (see tip, page 140)	45 mL

Dressing

1	clove garlic, minced	1
3 tbsp	extra virgin olive oil	45 mL
2 tbsp	freshly squeezed lemon juice	30 mL
1 tbsp	liquid honey	15 mL
1 tbsp	grainy mustard	15 mL

1. *Salad:* In a large bowl, toss together greens, bacon and cranberries.
2. *Dressing:* In a small bowl, whisk together garlic, oil, lemon juice, honey and mustard.
3. Just before serving, drizzle salad with dressing and top with goat cheese and walnuts.

Italian Salad

Makes 6 to 8 servings

St. Louis is quite close to Kansas City, and we visit there often. Its Little Italy area serves the best Italian fare in six states. This is our adaptation of the very popular Italian salad.

Make Ahead

Prepare the dressing, cover and refrigerate overnight. Bring to room temperature and whisk well before use. Wait to dress the salad until just before serving.

Salad

1	head romaine lettuce, torn into bite-size pieces	1
1	head iceberg lettuce, torn into bite-size pieces	1
1	jar (7.5 oz/213 mL) marinated artichoke hearts, drained and chopped	1
1	jar (4 oz/128 mL) diced pimentos, drained	1
1	red onion, thinly sliced	1
½ cup	freshly grated Parmesan cheese	125 mL

Dressing

½ cup	extra virgin olive oil	125 mL
⅓ cup	red wine vinegar	75 mL
	Salt and freshly ground black pepper	

1. *Salad:* In a large bowl, toss together romaine, iceberg lettuce, artichokes, pimentos, red onion and Parmesan.

2. *Dressing:* In a small bowl, whisk together oil and vinegar. Season to taste with salt and pepper.

3. Just before serving, pour dressing over salad and toss to coat.

Variation

Add toasted garlic cheese croutons and/or diced hard salami or pepperoni to the salad.

Sweet Endings and Hot Drinks

Elegant Chocolate Fondue

Makes about 4 cups (1 L)

If you like dark chocolate, this is the fondue for you. Serve with strawberries, banana slices, pirouette cookies and/or pound cake cubes.

Tip

Make an elegant evening even more tasty by serving a selection of dessert wines. This fondue is rich and dark enough to balance the flavor of dark red wines or Champagne.

	Nonstick baking spray	
8 oz	unsweetened chocolate, chopped	250 g
½ cup	unsalted butter, cut into pieces	125 mL
¾ cup	heavy or whipping (35%) cream	175 mL
¾ cup	half-and-half (10%) cream	175 mL
2½ cups	confectioners' (icing) sugar	625 mL
2 to 3 tbsp	coffee- or chocolate-flavored liqueur (optional)	30 to 45 mL

1. Spray one slow cooker stoneware with baking spray. Add chocolate and butter, stirring to combine.

2. Cover and cook on High for 1 hour or until melted. Stir well. Stir in heavy cream and half-and-half cream. Gradually stir in sugar. Cover and cook on Low for 30 minutes or until hot. Stir in liqueur to taste (if using). Turn to Warm for serving.

Simply Scrumptious Chocolate Fondue

Makes about 2 cups (500 mL)

When you serve this fantastic chocolate fondue, your kids will beg to stay at the table and will talk and giggle as they eat dessert. Serve with graham crackers, large marshmallows, strawberries, banana slices, pound cake cubes and/or angel food cake cubes.

Tip

If the fondue becomes too thick, stir in more cream.

	Nonstick baking spray	
12 oz	semisweet chocolate chips (2 cups/500 mL)	375 g
2 cups	miniature marshmallows	500 mL
¾ cup	heavy or whipping (35%) cream	175 mL

1. Spray one slow cooker stoneware with baking spray. Add chocolate chips, marshmallows and cream, stirring to combine.

2. Cover and cook on High for 1 hour, stirring halfway through, until melted. Turn to Warm for serving.

Variations

Rocky Road Fondue: Just before serving, stir in an additional ½ cup (125 mL) miniature marshmallows and ½ cup (125 mL) chopped roasted peanuts.

Chocolate Mint Fondue: Just before serving, stir in 1 tsp (5 mL) mint or peppermint extract or 2 to 3 tbsp (30 to 45 mL) crème de menthe liqueur.

Chocolate Peanut Butter Fondue: Add ½ cup (125 mL) peanut butter with the chocolate chips.

Coconut White Chocolate Fondue

Makes about 3 cups (750 mL)

This elegant fondue is perfect for an open house or a wedding or baby shower. Serve with angel food cake cubes, toasted pound cake cubes, strawberries, banana slices, pineapple pieces and/ or graham crackers.

Tips

White chocolate contains cocoa butter as a key ingredient, but no cocoa solids or chocolate liquor. Look for packages of bars or squares in the baking section of the grocery store. You may also find vanilla confections, so read the label — if it doesn't contain cocoa butter, it's not white chocolate and will not work well in this recipe.

Canned cream of coconut is commonly sold for cocktails and can be found in the mixed drink section of your grocery store. It should not be confused with coconut milk.

	Nonstick baking spray	
12 oz	vanilla baking chips (2 cups/500 mL)	375 g
6 oz	white chocolate (see tip, at left), chopped	175 g
Pinch	salt	Pinch
1 cup	heavy or whipping (35%) cream	250 mL
½ cup	cream of coconut	125 mL
2 tbsp	unsalted butter	30 mL
½ cup	sweetened flaked coconut	125 mL

1. Spray one slow cooker stoneware with baking spray. Add vanilla chips, white chocolate, salt, cream, cream of coconut and butter, stirring to combine.

2. Cover and cook on Low for 2 to 3 hours, stirring once every hour, until melted and smooth. Stir in coconut. Turn to Warm for serving.

Creamy Caramel Fondue

Makes about 1½ cups (375 mL)

When it comes to dessert fondues, everyone thinks of chocolate, so why not mix it up and make a caramel fondue? Serve with apple slices, pound cake cubes, doughnut holes and/or marshmallows.

Tips

Host a dessert party and serve three different fondues — this one, a chocolate fondue (page 164 or 165) and the Coconut White Chocolate Fondue (page 166).

If you can find an 11-oz (330 g) bag of caramel bits (such as Kraft Caramel Bits) that are not individually wrapped, feel free to use them in place of the soft caramels.

	Nonstick baking spray	
14 oz	soft caramels (2⅓ cups/575 mL)	400 g
½ cup	miniature marshmallows	125 mL
½ cup	heavy or whipping (35%) cream	125 mL
2 tbsp	strong brewed coffee	30 mL
1 tsp	vanilla extract	5 mL

1. Spray one slow cooker stoneware with baking spray. Add caramels, marshmallows, cream, coffee and vanilla, stirring to combine.

2. Cover and cook on High for 1 to 2 hours, stirring every 30 minutes, until melted and smooth. Turn to Warm for serving.

Variation

Substitute 2 tbsp (30 mL) dark rum for the coffee.

Cheesecake Fondue

Makes about 5½ cups (1.375 L)

Rich vanilla cheesecake turned into a warm, creamy fondue is the perfect dip for grilled fruit (see tip, below). You could also serve it with graham crackers, strawberries and/or banana slices.

Tip

To grill fruit to serve with this fondue, preheat barbecue grill to medium. Cut firm but ripe peaches, nectarines or pears (especially Bosc or Anjou pears) in half and cut away pit or core. Peel pineapple, cut out core and cut into 1-inch (2.5 cm) thick rings. Thread berries or smaller pieces of cut fruit onto skewers. If desired, brush fruit lightly with melted butter. Grill fruit, turning once, until just hot and attractive grill marks are evident.

	Nonstick baking spray	
1 lb	cream cheese, softened	500 g
1	can (14 oz or 300 mL) sweetened condensed milk	1
1 cup	miniature marshmallows	250 mL
1 cup	heavy or whipping (35%) cream	250 mL
2 tsp	vanilla extract	10 mL

1. Spray one slow cooker stoneware with baking spray.

2. In a large bowl, using an electric mixer on medium-high speed, beat cream cheese and milk until smooth. Transfer to prepared stoneware.

3. Cover and cook on Low for 1 hour, stirring halfway through. Stir in marshmallows, cream and vanilla. Cover and cook on Low for 1 hour or until melted and smooth. Stir until smooth. Turn to Warm for serving.

Amaretto Cream Fondue

Makes about 1¾ cups (425 mL)

We love to throw dessert parties, filling each of the stoneware vessels with a different fondue. Set out a wide array of dippers — pound cake cubes, angel food cake cubes, strawberries, long-stemmed maraschino cherries, fresh sweet cherries and/or shortbread cookies — and let the fun begin!

Tips

Cherries are perfectly complemented by the almond flavor in this fondue. Maraschino cherries should be drained and patted dry. If you use fresh cherries, caution diners about the pits.

For an elegant ice cream bar, serve this fondue over scoops of vanilla or chocolate ice cream. Add fresh peach slices to vanilla sundaes and maraschino cherries to chocolate sundaes.

	Nonstick baking spray	
12 oz	white chocolate (see tip, page 166), chopped	375 g
½ cup	heavy or whipping (35%) cream	125 mL
¼ cup	amaretto	60 mL
½ tsp	almond extract	2 mL

1. Spray one slow cooker stoneware with baking spray. Add white chocolate, cream, amaretto and almond extract, stirring to combine.

2. Cover and cook on High for 30 to 60 minutes, stirring halfway through, until melted. Turn to Warm for serving.

Variation

Chocolate Amaretto Fondue: Substitute semisweet chocolate for the white chocolate.

Praline Dip

Makes about 2$\frac{1}{2}$ cups (625 mL)

Both of us love pralines, so we make this dip often. Serve with apple slices, banana slices, pound cake cubes, marshmallows and/or chocolate-covered pretzels.

Tip

Toasting pecans intensifies their flavor. Spread chopped pecans in a single layer on a baking sheet. Bake at 350°F (180°C) for 5 to 7 minutes or until lightly browned. Let cool.

	Nonstick baking spray	
1 cup	firmly packed brown sugar	250 mL
$\frac{1}{4}$ tsp	ground cinnamon	1 mL
1	can (14 oz or 300 mL) sweetened condensed milk	1
$\frac{1}{4}$ cup	unsalted butter	60 mL
$\frac{1}{4}$ cup	light (white or golden) corn syrup	60 mL
$\frac{1}{2}$ cup	miniature marshmallows	125 mL
$\frac{1}{2}$ cup	chopped pecans, toasted (see tip, at left)	125 mL

1. Spray one slow cooker stoneware with baking spray. Add brown sugar, cinnamon, milk, butter and corn syrup, stirring to combine.

2. Cover and cook on High for 1 to 2 hours or until butter is melted and dip is hot. Stir in marshmallows. Cover and cook on High for 30 minutes or until marshmallows are melted. Turn to Warm for serving. Just before serving, stir in pecans.

Hot Fudge Sauce

Makes about 3 cups (750 mL)

This luscious sauce is truly a family favorite. In fact, when Kathy's family gathers for holidays and birthdays, everyone goes back for seconds.

Tips

If you prefer a thinner sauce, add more cream.

Adding a small amount of espresso or coffee is a good way to intensify the flavor of chocolate. No one will detect a coffee flavor, but everyone will exclaim how great the sauce tastes. If desired, you can omit the espresso powder.

¼ cup	unsalted butter	60 mL
12 oz	semisweet chocolate chips (2 cups/500 mL)	375 g
1 tsp	instant espresso powder	5 mL
1	can (14 oz or 300 mL) sweetened condensed milk	1
¼ cup	light (white or golden) corn syrup	60 mL
¼ cup	heavy or whipping (35%) cream	60 mL

1. Rub one slow cooker stoneware with butter, then place the remaining butter in the stoneware. Stir in chocolate chips, espresso powder, milk, corn syrup and cream.

2. Cover and cook on High for 30 to 60 minutes, stirring halfway through, until melted. Turn to Warm for serving.

Bananas Foster

Makes 8 servings

A classic brown sugar and butter sauce transforms bananas into a glorious, elegant dessert. We seek it out every time we travel to New Orleans.

Tip

Serve bananas Foster over scoops of vanilla ice cream, just as they do in New Orleans. Or, for a change of pace, serve over slices of pound cake.

1 cup	packed brown sugar	250 mL
¼ tsp	ground cinnamon	1 mL
½ cup	unsalted butter, cut into pieces	125 mL
4	ripe bananas, cut into 1-inch (2.5 cm) slices	4
¼ cup	dark rum	60 mL

1. In one slow cooker stoneware, combine brown sugar, cinnamon and butter.

2. Cover and cook on Low for 30 to 60 minutes or until butter is melted. Stir well to dissolve sugar.

3. Add bananas, stirring gently to coat. Stir in rum. Cover and cook on Low for 15 minutes or until bananas are warm. Turn to Warm for serving.

Cherries Jubilee

**Makes 5 cups
(1.25 L)**

This classic dessert is generally credited to the famous 19th-century chef Auguste Escoffier. It is said he first served it in honor of Queen Victoria's Golden Jubilee.

Tips

Dried cherries provide an intense cherry flavor in this recipe, but if you wish, you can omit them and use 3 cans of dark sweet cherries. Reduce the sugar to ¼ cup (60 mL).

Serve warm cherries jubilee over vanilla ice cream or slices of pound cake.

2	cans (each 15 to 19 oz/ 425 to 540 mL) pitted dark sweet cherries in heavy syrup	2
½ cup	dried cherries	125 mL
½ cup	granulated sugar	125 mL
¼ cup	orange juice	60 mL
¼ tsp	almond extract	1 mL
2 tbsp	cornstarch	30 mL
3 tbsp	cold water	45 mL
⅓ cup	Kirsch or brandy	75 mL

1. In one slow cooker stoneware, stir together canned cherries with syrup, dried cherries, sugar, orange juice and almond extract.

2. Cover and cook on Low for 3 hours.

3. In a small bowl, stir together cornstarch and cold water; stir into stoneware. Cover and cook on High for 30 minutes or until thickened. Stir in Kirsch. Turn to Warm for serving.

Apple Crisp

Apple orchards are prolific in the midwestern United States, where we hail from, so we've had ample opportunity to perfect a great slow cooker apple crisp recipe.

Tips

Select tart baking apples, such as Granny Smith, Empire, Jonathan or Braeburn.

Serve with a scoop of vanilla or cinnamon-flavored ice cream. To make serving ice cream to a crowd easier, line a baking sheet with parchment paper. Place scoops of ice cream on the tray and set the tray in the freezer so the scoops can refreeze.

	Nonstick baking spray	
7½ cups	sliced peeled baking apples	1.875 L
½ cup	sweetened dried cranberries	125 mL
¾ cup	packed brown sugar	175 mL
½ cup	quick-cooking or large-flake (old-fashioned) rolled oats	125 mL
2 tsp	ground cinnamon	10 mL
⅔ cup	cold unsalted butter, cut into pieces	150 mL

1. Spray one slow cooker stoneware with baking spray. Add apples and cranberries, tossing gently to combine.

2. In a medium bowl, combine brown sugar, oats and cinnamon. Using your fingertips or a pastry blender, cut in butter until mixture resembles coarse crumbs. Sprinkle evenly over apple mixture.

3. Cover and cook on Low for 4 to 5 hours or on High for 2 to 2½ hours, until apples are tender. Turn to Warm for serving.

Peach Crumble

Makes 8 to 10 servings

Crisps and crumbles are go-to desserts for the slow cooker. Without any fuss, you can present a crowd-pleasing treat every time. Serve with a scoop of vanilla ice cream.

Tip

Toasting pecans intensifies their flavor. Spread chopped pecans in a single layer on a baking sheet. Bake at 350°F (180°C) for 5 to 7 minutes or until lightly browned. Let cool.

	Nonstick baking spray	
2 lbs	frozen sliced peaches	1 kg
¾ cup	granulated sugar	175 mL
4 tsp	instant or quick-cooking tapioca	20 mL
1 tsp	ground cinnamon	5 mL
¼ tsp	ground nutmeg	1 mL
2 tsp	freshly squeezed lemon juice	10 mL

Topping

¾ cup	large-flake (old-fashioned) rolled oats	175 mL
½ cup	packed brown sugar	125 mL
¼ cup	all-purpose flour	60 mL
6 tbsp	cold unsalted butter, cut into pieces	90 mL
1 cup	chopped pecans, toasted (see tip, at left)	250 mL

1. Spray one slow cooker stoneware with baking spray.

2. In a medium bowl, combine peaches, sugar, tapioca, cinnamon, nutmeg and lemon juice. Spoon into prepared stoneware.

3. *Topping:* In another bowl, combine oats, brown sugar and flour. Using your fingertips or a pastry blender, cut in butter until mixture resembles coarse crumbs. Sprinkle evenly over peach mixture. Sprinkle with pecans.

4. Cover and cook on Low for 4 to 6 hours or on High for 2 to 3 hours, until peaches are tender. Turn to Warm for serving.

Strawberry Rhubarb Dessert

Makes 8 servings

Dollops of dough, baked like biscuits or scones, make the crust for this dessert. It reminds Kathy of cobblers her mom and grandma used to make when she was growing up.

Tips

Fresh rhubarb is readily available, especially in the spring. Trim off the leaves and roots, leaving just the stalk, then chop it. For this recipe, you'll need 10 to 12 oz (300 to 375 g) of rhubarb to make 2 cups (500 mL) chopped.

Thawed frozen rhubarb may be substitute for fresh in this recipe.

The baked crust will be more flaky if you use very cold butter and cream.

- Baking sheet, lined with parchment paper

	Nonstick baking spray	
4 cups	strawberries, hulled and cut in half	1 L
2 cups	chopped rhubarb (1-inch/2.5 cm pieces)	500 mL
¾ cup	granulated sugar	175 mL
¼ cup	all-purpose flour	60 mL
2 tbsp	cornstarch	30 mL
Pinch	salt	Pinch

Crust

1 cup	all-purpose flour	250 mL
4 tsp	granulated sugar, divided	20 mL
1½ tsp	baking powder	7 mL
½ tsp	salt	2 mL
3 tbsp	very cold unsalted butter	45 mL
⅔ cup	very cold heavy or whipping (35%) cream	150 mL

1. Spray one slow cooker stoneware with baking spray.

2. In a medium bowl, combine strawberries, rhubarb, sugar, flour, cornstarch and salt. Transfer to prepared stoneware.

3. Cover and cook on Low for 4 to 5 hours or on High for 2 to 2½ hours, until fruit is tender. Turn to Warm for serving.

4. About 30 minutes before serving, preheat oven to 400°F (200°C).

Tips

If desired, top each dessert with a dollop of sweetened whipped cream or a scoop of ice cream.

Create a shortcake-like dessert by slicing each crust dollop in half and topping the slices with the strawberry-rhubarb mixture and whipped cream.

5. *Crust:* In a medium bowl, whisk together flour, 3 tsp (45 mL) of the sugar, baking powder and salt. Using your fingertips or a pastry blender, cut in butter until mixture resembles coarse crumbs. Using a fork, stir in cream until a soft dough forms.

6. Divide dough into 8 dollops and place about 2 inches (5 cm) apart on prepared baking sheet. Sprinkle the remaining sugar evenly over dollops of dough.

7. Bake for 18 to 20 minutes or until golden brown.

8. To serve, spoon fruit mixture into bowls and place a crust dollop on top of each. Serve warm.

Hot German Wine Punch

**Makes about
6 cups (1.5 L)**

On our last trip to New
York City, we enjoyed
a wonderful lunch with
our good friends Karen
Adler and Judith Fertig
at Café Sabarsky at the
Neue Galerie. We all
enjoyed cups of their
great *gluhwein* — a
mulled wine. That
fantastic lunch inspired
this recipe. We
encourage you to pour
a cup and enjoy time
with your friends.

Tips

Place the cloves in a fine-
mesh spice ball so it's easier
to remove them.

For an attractive
presentation, float thin slices
of orange and/or lemon over
the wine just before serving.

½ cup	packed brown sugar	125 mL
2	2- to 3-inch (5 to 7.5 cm) cinnamon sticks	2
2 to 3	whole cloves	2 to 3
2	bottles (each 750 mL) dry red wine	2
	Juice of 1 orange	
	Juice of 1 lemon	

1. In one slow cooker stoneware, combine brown sugar, cinnamon sticks, cloves, wine, orange juice and lemon juice.

2. Cover and cook on High for 2 to 3 hours or until hot. Discard cinnamon sticks and cloves. Turn to Warm for serving.

Holiday Cranberry Punch

Makes 8 cups (2 L)

Holiday gatherings at Kathy's house mean a hot punch is kept warm in the slow cooker all day, so it is ready to serve as friends and family drop by.

½ cup	packed brown sugar	125 mL
2	2- to 3-inch (5 to 7.5 cm) cinnamon sticks	2
½ tsp	whole cloves	2 mL
4 cups	cranberry juice cocktail	1 L
4 cups	unsweetened pineapple juice	1 L
½	orange, thinly sliced	½

1. In one slow cooker stoneware, combine brown sugar, cinnamon sticks, cloves, cranberry cocktail and pineapple juice.

2. Cover and cook on High for 2 to 3 hours or until hot. Discard cinnamon sticks and cloves. Add sliced orange. Turn to Warm for serving.

Variation

Stir in ¼ to ½ cup (60 to 125 mL) cranberry-flavored liqueur or vodka just before serving.

Our Favorite Hot Cider

Makes 8 cups (2 L)

After a family trip to the local orchard and cider mill, we love to prepare mulled cider, then leisurely enjoy a mug while we remember the fun of the day. We hope you and your family will build wonderful memories around mugs of hot cider too.

Tips

Place the cloves in a fine-mesh spice ball so it's easier to remove them.

Add ½ tsp (2 mL) whole allspice berries with the cinnamon and cloves.

Some like sweet mulled cider; others like it tart. Adjust the sugar to your personal preference.

½ cup	packed brown sugar (or to taste)	125 mL
2	2- to 3-inch (5 to 7.5 cm) cinnamon sticks	2
1 tsp	whole cloves	5 mL
8 cups	unsweetened apple cider	2 L

1. In one slow cooker stoneware, combine brown sugar, cinnamon sticks, cloves and cider.

2. Cover and cook on High for 2 to 3 hours or until hot. Discard cinnamon sticks and cloves. Turn to Warm for serving.

Hot Cocoa for a Crowd

**Makes about
7 cups (1.75 L)**

Skiing, ice skating,
playing in the snow,
cutting down Christmas
trees, sledding — any
time friends gather
for fun in the cold, hot
cocoa is sure to follow.
Fill the slow cooker
before you go outside,
and it will be hot and
waiting for you when
you return home.

Tip

For fun toppings, set out
bowls of marshmallows,
whipped cream and/or
unsweetened cocoa powder.
Add peppermint sticks
for stirring.

⅔ cup	granulated sugar	150 mL
½ cup	unsweetened cocoa powder	125 mL
Pinch	salt	Pinch
⅓ cup	water	75 mL
6 cups	milk	1.5 L
1 tsp	vanilla extract	5 mL

1. In a small saucepan, whisk together sugar, cocoa and
   salt. Whisk in water. Cook over medium heat, stirring
   constantly, until sugar is completely dissolved and
   mixture begins to simmer.

2. Pour cocoa mixture into one slow cooker stoneware.
   Stir in milk.

3. Cover and cook on High for 2 to 3 hours or until hot. Stir
   in vanilla. Turn to Warm for serving.

Variation

Stir in 2 to 4 tbsp (30 to 60 mL) crème de cacao,
peppermint schnapps, crème de menthe, Kahlúa or
another favorite liqueur just before serving.

Vanilla Latte

Makes 6⅔ cups (1.65 L)

This latte is half milk and half coffee — and we love it. You're sure to serve it often.

Tips

Vanilla syrup is available in larger grocery stores, often near the coffee, and at coffee shops.

Have you been told to avoid fresh milk when slow cooking? It's true — if a recipe cooks all day on Low, the milk may well curdle. However, milk works well in recipes with shorter cooking times of up to 3 hours. Do not try to hold on the Warm setting for longer than 2 hours.

Use decaffeinated coffee to prepare this recipe, if desired.

3 cups	milk	750 mL
⅔ cup	vanilla syrup	150 mL
3 cups	hot freshly brewed double-strength coffee	750 mL

1. In one slow cooker stoneware, combine milk and vanilla syrup.
2. Cover and cook on High for $1\frac{1}{2}$ hours or until hot. Stir in coffee. Turn to Warm for serving.

Caramel Latte

**Makes about
5 cups (1.25 L)**

Sometimes we need to make a point of finding time to relax and enjoy our friends. Sampling this tasty, inviting drink may be just the excuse you need to invite them over.

Tips

Cutting calories? Use skim milk and fat-free half-and-half.

Be sure to use very strong coffee for this recipe and the other lattes (pages 182 and 184).

Use decaffeinated coffee to prepare this recipe, if desired.

¼ cup	packed brown sugar	60 mL
1 cup	milk	250 mL
½ cup	half-and-half (10%) cream	125 mL
⅓ cup	caramel sundae syrup	75 mL
3 cups	hot freshly brewed double-strength coffee	750 mL

1. In one slow cooker stoneware, combine brown sugar, milk, cream and caramel syrup.

2. Cover and cook on High for 2 hours or until hot and sugar has dissolved. Stir in coffee. Turn to Warm for serving.

Gingerbread Latte

No need to stop at
a fancy coffee shop
when you want flavored
coffee. This one is
delightful all fall and
winter — it's one of our
favorites.

Tips

Top mugs of the hot latte
with whipped cream and a
light dusting of cinnamon.

Use decaffeinated coffee
to prepare this recipe,
if desired.

¼ cup	water	60 mL
½ cup	confectioners' (icing) sugar	125 mL
2 tsp	ground ginger	10 mL
1 tsp	ground cinnamon	5 mL
¼ tsp	ground cloves	1 mL
3 cups	milk	750 mL
2 cups	hot freshly brewed double-strength coffee	500 mL
2 tsp	vanilla extract	10 mL

1. In a small microwave-safe glass bowl or 2-cup (500 mL) glass measuring cup, microwave water on High for 30 seconds or until hot. Stir in sugar, ginger, cinnamon and cloves. Microwave on High for 30 seconds or until boiling. Stir to dissolve sugar and spices. Pour into one slow cooker stoneware. Stir in milk.

2. Cover and cook on High for 2 to 3 hours or until hot. Stir in coffee and vanilla. Turn to Warm for serving.

Internet Support and Mail Order Sources

The Electrified Cooks, LLC: www.electrifiedcooks.com
Our blog, filled with recipes, tips, classes and more:
www.pluggedintocooking.com

Select Brands: www.selectbrands.com

Babycakes®: www.thebabycakesshop.com

Penzeys Spices (fresh spices): www.penzeys.com

Library and Archives Canada Cataloguing in Publication

Moore, Kathy, 1954–
    Triple slow cooker entertaining : 100+ recipes & 30 party
plans / Kathy Moore & Roxanne Wyss.

Includes index.
ISBN 978-0-7788-0444-4

    1. Electric cooking, Slow. 2. Entertaining. 3. Parties—
Planning. I. Wyss, Roxanne II. Title.

TX827.M65 2012   641.5'884   C2012-905431-3

Index